Survey of Corporate Contributions, 1989 Edition

(An Analysis of Data for the Calendar Year 1987)

by Linda Cardillo Platzer
and
Maureen Nevin Duffy

This report is based on data from the Annual Survey of Corporate Contributions,
which is sponsored by The Conference Board and the Council for Aid to Education.

Contents

From the President

Last year, charitable contributions plateaued and now may have begun to slide backwards. The growth rate of the 1970s and early 1980s has begun to erode. The response from major corporations to this *Survey of Corporate Contributions* points to a decline in 1987 and possible further declines in 1988. The Conference Board's *Survey of Corporate Contributions*, now in its twenty-second edition, provides executives with a detailed, comprehensive overview of contributions practices based on information provided by 328 firms. As a budgeting and planning tool, this report enables executives to assess their programs against those of other firms in their own industry, with the same income or asset size, or in their region of the country, and to evaluate national trends.

This report includes charts that present important highlights graphically and succinctly. Trends in noncash contributions, corporate assistance, foundation grants, and corporate priorities, for example, are easier to follow through such charts.

The Conference Board is grateful to the contributions executives who participate every year in this survey. Their sustained support is essential to the quality of the information we are able to report.

PRESTON TOWNLEY
President

Highlights

In 1987, corporate charitable contributions by the largest U.S. corporations continued a pattern begun in the mid-eighties of moderate growth, reduced expectations, and dependence on noncash contributions to supplement corporate giving programs.

The Council for Aid to Education, cosponsor of this report, estimates that total corporate contributions remained at $4.6 billion in 1987 (in current dollars). This represents a drop of nearly 4% from 1986 levels.

This report is based on the responses of 328 companies surveyed by The Conference Board regarding their corporate contributions for 1987. The major findings of the 1987 survey were:

• Total contributions reported by companies participating for two consecutive years (a matched sample) grew approximately 5% between 1986 and 1987. After more than a decade of yearly growth rates that ranged between 13% and 26%, contributions increases among the nation's leading corporate donors in the last three years have slowed to between 3% and 7% per year.

• In most industries, corporate giving has not kept pace with increases in corporate profits. Companies in the manufacturing sector, for example, reported an aggregate increase of 20% in corporate profits, compared to a 4% increase in corporate giving. As a result, the ratios of contributions to pretax income were generally low.

• For the fourth year in a row, over 20% of corporate charitable giving was in noncash form—gifts of securities, company product, property or equipment. Noncash giving was particularly prominent among the largest donors (programs of $6 million or more), where noncash contributions accounted for one-quarter of reported donations. One extraordinary gift of property—valued at nearly $90 million—accounted for a large part of the increase reported by matched-sample companies. Gifts of company product—in particular, food, pharmaceuticals, computer equipment, and books—as well as gifts of property such as real estate, have become essential elements in many companies' contributions budgets.

Giving to Education. In 1987, 37% of total contributions went to educational institutions, a level consistent with the range over most of the last ten years. (An extraordinary gift of property in 1986 lifted the overall percentage donated to education to an exceptionally high level, so that the drop to 37%—from 42.9%—appeared more dramatic than it actually was. The contribution percentage to education in 1985, for example, was 38.3%.)

Giving to health and human services as a percentage of total contributions continued a 10-year downward trend—from 36.9% in 1978 to 27% in 1987.

Civic and community activites grew slightly as a percentage of total giving—from 13% to 14%. Property gifts accounted for some of the resurgence in giving in this category.

Contributions to the *arts* dropped slightly to 11% from 12%, but remained within the range that has been maintained over the last decade.

Contributions to *"other"* organizations were exceptionally high at 11% because of the $90-million property gift, which accounted for approximately half of the giving in this category. In addition to the property gift, however, were sizable donations of product by pharmaceutical companies to organizations providing overseas relief.

Sample

The *Survey of Corporate Contributions* studies the contributions practices of companies with major charitable giving programs—programs which donate at least $100,000 annually—which, in general, operate according to established guidelines for giving; and have some *institutional* continuity. Such major programs tend to be found among the largest companies, and therefore, the sample for the survey is based on lists of the largest U.S. corporations.

The Conference Board asked 1,200 top U.S. firms to participate in its 1987 *Survey of Corporate Contributions*. Questionnaires were sent to the companies that appeared on the 1988 *Fortune* 500 Industrials list of the country's largest manufacturers and to those on the *Fortune* 500 Service list of the largest nonmanufacturing firms. An additional 200 companies, which were identified from published lists of the leading companies in each major industry sector, were also polled. Because the survey has been administered annually since 1974, many companies participate regularly, providing a basis for historical comparisons company-by-company. In the 1987 Survey, 78% of the respondents had also participated in the 1986 survey.

A total of 328 companies returned the questionnaire for 1987—a response rate of 27 percent. The aggregate contributions reported by these companies amount to 35% of the total contributions reported to the Internal Revenue Service by all U.S. corporations. (See Appendix Table 1 on page 35.)

Respondent Profile

The participants in the survey are leaders in corporate contributions. More than half of the companies responding to the 1987 survey each had contributions budgets that exceeded $1 million (Table A-1). Fifty-five percent of the respondents are manufacturing firms. Of these, 86% appear on the *Fortune* 500 list and over three-quarters reported worldwide sales of over $1 billion in 1987.

The remaining respondents are in the service sector, with nearly 70% appearing on the *Fortune* Service 500 list.

Other characteristics of the respondent population are described in Tables A-2 through A-5.

Survey Administration

The questionnaire used to collect 1987 data was adapted from the 1986 questionnaire to make it shorter and less complicated to complete, but to retain year-to-year comparability of data. The questionnaire requested information concerning company direct giving and company foundation programs, cash and noncash giving, overseas giving, giving to subcategories of the five major beneficiary groups (for definitions, see page 20), and corporate assistance expenditures. Financial information about the company's sales, income, and assets was obtained from the company's annual report or other published data. The questionnaire was mailed in March 1988, and addressed to a named contributions executive when a name was known. If no name was available, the covering letter was sent to the "Corporate Contributions Executive." Nonrespondents were sent a follow-up letter in April.

This year's report reflects a lower number of participants and in large measure this is due to a decrease in the number of major charitable contributors—a reduction caused largely by mergers and acquisitions. In other instances, reduced staffing has made it more difficult for companies to respond because of fewer personnel available to answer the questionnaire. In some industry categories, the number of respondents for 1987 was too low to draw any meaningful conclusions about the industry. To report information for those companies, a new industry category was introduced in all the industry tables in this edition of the survey. "Other Manufacturing" is a composite category that includes primary metal industries, fabricated metal products, and stone, clay and glass products.

Table A-1: Profile of Participating Companies by Size of Contributions Program, 1985 to 1987

Program Size	1987		1986		1985	
	Number	Percent	Number	Percent	Number	Percent
Less than $500,000	74	23%	87	23%	116	27%
$500,000 to $1 million	62	19	72	19	79	18
$1 million to $5 million	111	34	128	35	164	37
$5 million and over	81	25	85	23	80	18
Total	328	100%	372	100%	439	100%

Totals may not add to 100 percent due to rounding.

Table A-2: Survey Participants—
Grouped by Worldwide Sales, 1987

Worldwide Sales	Manufacturing Companies		Selected Nonmanufacturing Companies[1]	
	Number	Percent	Number	Percent
Below $250 million	3	2%	—	—
$250-500 million	8	5	1	4%
$500 million-1 billion	22	14	5	22
$1 billion-2.5 billion	44	27	7	30
$2.5 billion-5 billion	33	20	5	22
$5 billion and over	51	32	5	22
Total	161	100%	23	100%

[1]Excludes banks, insurance companies, telecommunications and utilities companies, which are grouped by Assets in Table A-3.

Table A-3: Survey Participants in Banking, Insurance, Telephone, Gas and Electric Utilities,
Grouped by Worldwide Assets, 1987

Worldwide Assets	Banking		Insurance		Telephone, Gas and Electric Utilities	
	Number	Percent	Number	Percent	Number	Percent
Under $250 million	—	—	—	—	—	—
$250-$500 million	—	—	1	3%	—	—
$500 million-1 billion	—	—	2	7	5	10%
$1 billion-2.5 billion	4	13%	3	10	9	19
$2.5 billion-5 billion	3	9	7	23	9	19
$5 billion-10 billion	10	31	7	23	11	23
$10 billion and over	15	47	10	33	14	29
Total	32	100%	30	100%	48	100%

Table A-4: Comparison of Manufacturing Companies in 1987 Survey with Those in the *Fortune* 500 List — Companies Grouped by *Fortune* Ranking (Based on Total Worldwide Sales)

Company Rank	Number of Survey Respondents
Number 1- 100	63
101- 200	43
201- 300	21
301- 400	19
401- 500	7
Total	153

Table A-5: Comparison of Nonmanufacturing Companies in the 1987 Survey with Those on the *Fortune* Service 500 List—Companies Grouped by Industry Class

Industry Class (Top 500)	Number of Survey Respondents
Top 100 diversified service companies (ranked by sales)	10
Top 100 commercial banking companies (ranked by assets)	26
Top 50 savings institutions (ranked by assets)	3
Top 50 life insurance companies (ranked by assets)	15
Top 50 diversified financial companies (ranked by assets)	16
Top 50 retailing companies (ranked by sales)	4
Top 50 transportation companies (ranked by operating revenues)	4
Top 50 utilities (ranked by assets)	25
Total	103

Chapter 1
An Overview of 1987 Contributions Activity

Corporate charitable contributions in 1987 continued a pattern of slow growth—in real terms, less than 1% for all U.S. corporations—after three years, that appears characteristic of the second half of this decade in corporate giving. In the mid-1980s, many of the major oil companies—long the flag-bearers in corporate philanthropy—sharply reduced their contributions budgets in the wake of falling profits and giving levels have yet to recover. At the same time, a number of other corporations, also leaders in charitable contributions, underwent major institutional changes—in leadership, in size (the result of acquisitions or divestitures), and in corporate direction. The restructuring of Corporate America has, at the least, precipitated a *rethinking* of the role of the contributions budget, if not outright reductions.

Chart 1:
Corporate Contributions and Corporate Income Before Taxes in Current and Constant Dollars, 1972 to 1987

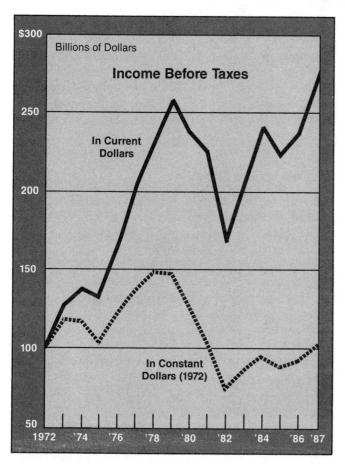

Source: U.S. Department of Commerce

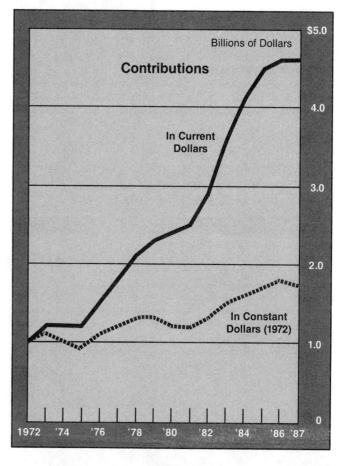

Source: Internal Revenue Service; 1985 and 1986 estimate by Council for Aid to Education.

In 1987, total corporate contributions by all U.S. corporations were estimated by the Council for Aid to Education to have stagnated at $4.6 billion, reflecting a drop of nearly 4% in constant dollars compared to 1986. (See Charts 1 and 2.) At the same time, corporate income before taxes posted a gain of nearly 13%, adjusted for inflation. Not since the early 1970s has corporate income before taxes grown faster than corporate contributions, and never before has corporate contributions lagged so far behind income growth. Both the pattern of the data displayed in Chart 2 and anecdotal reports from corporate contributions practitioners reveal a shift away from large annual increases in contributions budgets toward a more controlled, measured growth.

The Conference Board Survey measures changes in the magnitude of corporate giving among survey participants through a matched sample. Each survey year, the responses of a core group of companies are matched with their responses from the previous year to compare changes on a case-by-case basis. Among the matched-case respondents, total contributions in 1987 grew at a healthier pace than the overall corporate philanthropic community, advancing nearly 5 percent. Extraordinary noncash gifts, discussed later in this chapter, played a sizable role in that increase. In general, since 1985, survey matched-case companies have experienced a significant and abrupt change in the rate at which their contributions programs have grown. Between 1977 and 1984, contributions by those companies grew annually at double-digit rates, often over 20% per year. Since 1985, however, their contributions budget increases have slowed to 3% to 7% per year.

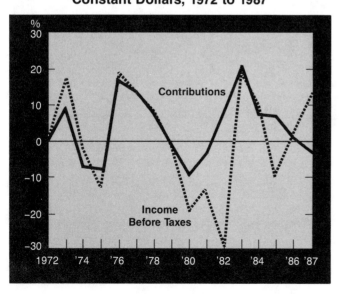

Chart 2:
Percentage Change In Contributions and Corporate Income Before Taxes in Constant Dollars, 1972 to 1987

The Outlook for Corporate Contributions

The immediate future for corporate contributions is one of moderation. In mid-1988 The Conference Board asked survey participants to anticipate their final 1988 contributions budgets. In the aggregate, respondents expected end-of-year figures to be approximately 4% lower than 1987 budgets (Chart 3 and Table 1). However, most of that decrease reflects the presence or absence of extraordinary noncash gifts, which are often unanticipated. Respondents tend to underestimate their final budgets because of these unpredictable additions to their programs.

A clearer picture of corporate expectations on giving emerges from the industry subcategories. For example, the substantial decrease expected in 1988 by companies in the electrical machinery and equipment industry (-23%) is the result of an extraordinarily large donation of property in 1987, which temporarily inflated total contributions and will probably not be repeated. The drop anticipated by insurance companies (-15%) is also the result of 1987 property donations. However, companies in this industry regularly make such donations and tend to underestimate or omit such gifts from their estimated budgets.

The aggregate figures for 1988 also show a decline (see Table 2) because many of those reporting decreases are among the largest companies participating in the survey. Of the top 75 donors in 1987 (companies with budgets of more than $6 million), 25 expected to reduce contributions in 1988, with decreases ranging from less than 1% to nearly 30 percent.

Most of the survey respondents, however, were anticipating positive change. Two-thirds of the companies reporting their final budgets for 1988 thought that they would be the same or higher than 1987, and half of those were planning increases of greater than 10 percent.

Cash and Noncash Giving

Cash is the primary form of corporate charitable contributions. In 1987, gifts of cash rose approximately 5% over 1986 levels and represented nearly four-fifths of all donations. The top-ranked company for cash contributions gave a total of $76.2 million, down from the high of $77.5 million in 1986. The median cash contribution, however, was up from $1.2 million to nearly $1.5 million. Among 1987 survey respondents, 36 companies each gave more than $10 million in the form of cash.

Since 1984, noncash charitable contributions—gifts of securities, company product, and property and equipment—have accounted for at least 20% of all corporate giving (see Charts 4 and 5). In the manufacturing sector, noncash donations are a particularly vital element of giving programs, representing 26% of total donations (see Chart 6).

The use of noncash gifts can often profoundly alter the magnitude of a company's total contributions, sometimes doubling or tripling the cash portion of a contributions budget. Such an effect can be seen most clearly in Table 3. Of the

75 top-ranked donors, 11 companies gave 50% or more in the form of noncash gifts; only 31 companies gave 100% cash. Whether these companies are doubling or tripling the *effectiveness* of their donations is an issue being debated, particularly by beneficiaries of corporate support and by companies that have neither appropriate products nor available properties to donate. What is clear is that noncash giving has become a well-established element in the repertoire of the corporate contributions manager.

In 1987, 11% of all contributions were company product donations; but in several industry groups, products (such as foods, pharmaceuticals, computer equipment, and books) constitute a much higher proportion of giving (see Table 4). Industry groups reporting the highest dollar values of products include: electrical machinery and equipment ($70

million); food, beverage and tobacco ($48 million); and pharmaceutical companies ($25 million). The largest amount reported by a single company was $20 million; but the median value for company product was $321,000. Approximately one-fifth of survey respondents reported product donations.

Product donations among matched-sample companies fell 8% between 1986 and 1987, but about one-half of the drop can be attributed to figures that did not make it into this report by deadline, rather than to cutbacks in such donations.

Property and surplus equipment donations accounted for $164 million—10% of 1987 contributions. Among the matched-sample companies such gifts advanced 30% over 1986 levels. However, more than half of the amount reported was the result of a *single* gift of property valued at nearly

Chart 3:
Anticipated Changes in 1988 Budgets, by Industry

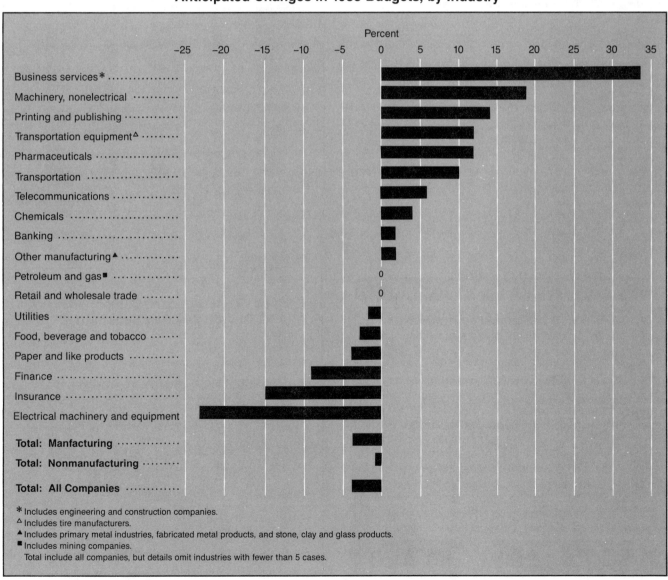

* Includes engineering and construction companies.
△ Includes tire manufacturers.
▲ Includes primary metal industries, fabricated metal products, and stone, clay and glass products.
■ Includes mining companies.
Total include all companies, but details omit industries with fewer than 5 cases.

$90 million. Such extraordinary gifts can and do radically alter the proportions of the various components of corporate contributions in a given year—not only the mix of cash and noncash, but also the distribution of contributions among the five categories of beneficiaries. But such changes are neither consistent nor predictable and can only be noted as aberrations, both for the individual company and for contributions activity in the aggregate.

Companies in three different industry groups made sizable donations of property and equipment in 1987—electrical machinery and equipment ($100 million); transportation equipment ($22 million); and insurance ($19 million). The median gift of property was $53,000, less than half the median property donation made in 1986.

Securities donations are a relatively rare form of corporate giving, typically accounting for less than 1% of all gifts. In 1987, only four companies reported such gifts, all in the financial services and insurance industries.

Corporate Assistance Expenditures

A number of companies supplement their charitable giving programs with additional support to nonprofit organizations. Such support is generally treated as a business expense rather than a charitable deduction, and quite often originates in company departments other than corporate contributions. Nevertheless, these expenses have fundamentally the same goals as charitable donations. In 1982, The Conference Board first defined such expenditures as "corporate assistance" and began to quantify the extent to which companies were making them. The expenditures that meet The Conference Board's definition of corporate assistance appear in the adjacent box.

Many companies find it difficult to track and quantify cor-

porate assistance activities. Much of the assistance is in noncash forms, such as the use of corporate facilities or the loan of company personnel, and often the expenses are not under the control of the contributions function. As a result, much of the information collected may be an understatement of what is actually taking place. It is possible, however, to identify broad trends and relative priorities in corporate assistance activities.

Approximately 40% (136) of the companies participating in the 1987 survey reported corporate assistance expenditures

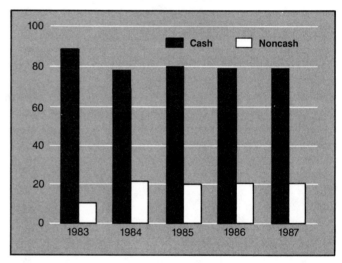

Chart 4:
**Cash and Noncash Giving
1983 to 1987**

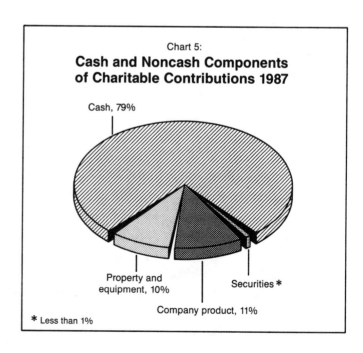

Chart 5:
**Cash and Noncash Components
of Charitable Contributions 1987**

Cash, 79%

Property and equipment, 10%

Securities *

Company product, 11%

* Less than 1%

Defining Corporate Assistance

In 1982, five major categories of expenditures to nonprofit groups, plus a sixth category covering administrative costs, were defined by The Conference Board as "corporate assistance expenditures."

The six categories encompass: (1) cash disbursements, such as "basic research" grants made by a company's R&D department to colleges and universities; support for public television and radio; monies paid for benefit events; or membership fees paid to nonprofit groups; (2) the loan of company personnel to nonprofit organizations for management or technical assistance; (3) product and property donations to nonprofit groups; (4) the use of corporate facilities (such as office or meeting space) or of services (such as printing or computer processing) by nonprofit groups; (5) loans, deposits, and investments for social purposes at below-market rates; and (6) the direct costs of administering the contributions function.

in addition to their charitable donations in 1987. Expenditures ranged in size from $1,000 to $24 million, with a median expenditure of $194,000, a drop of 17% from the 1986 median. The sum of a company's charitable contributions and corporate assistance activities constitute its total corporate social expenditures. (See Appendix Table 8B for a ranking of the top 75 donors in corporate social expenditures.) For the companies reporting to The Conference Board since 1982, corporate assistance activities have consistently accounted for approximately one dollar out of every five spent on social causes.

A summary of corporate assistance expenditures in 1987 appears in Table 6[1]. On the whole, median expenditures in each category were considerably higher than in 1986. The

[1]In 1987, 58 new companies reported corporate assistance activities, but 55 companies that had reported such expenditures in 1986 did not report any in 1987. Out of the total of 136 companies reporting corporate assistance expenditures in 1987, only 78 had also reported such expenditures in 1986. As a result, the matched sample for corporate assistance expenditures contains only 78 companies—too small to make any meaningful comparisons. Therefore, tables presenting corporate assistance expenditures are based only on 1987 figures and not on a direct comparison via the matched sample.

The Top Five Industry Leaders in Corporate Assistance Expenditures

Total Corporate Assistance ($ Millions)

Food, beverage, and tobacco	$60
Electrical machinery and equipment	$34
Chemicals	$15
Insurance	$13
Utilities	$11

Median Corporate Assistance ($ Thousands)

Petroleum and gas	$700
Electrical machinery and equipment	$612
Food, beverage, and tobacco	$550
Chemicals	$435
Pharmaceuticals	$297

Corporate Assistance as Percent of Total Contributions

Utilities	45%
Food, beverage, and tobacco	42
Machinery, nonelectrical	30
Banking	25
Chemicals	24

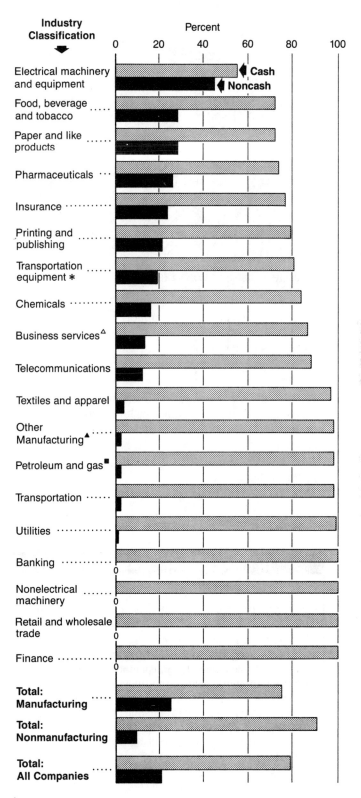

Chart 6:
Cash and Noncash Contributions by Industry, 1987

* Includes tire manufacturers.
△ Includes engineering and construction companies.
▲ Includes primary metal industries, fabricated metal products, and stone, clay and glass products.
■ Includes mining companies.

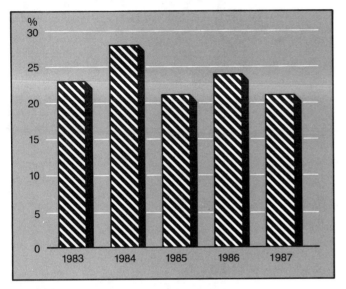

Chart 7:

**Corporate Assistance as a Percent
of Total Contributions, 1983 to 1987**

median for noncharitable cash disbursements, the largest category of corporate assistance expenditures, advanced from $115,000 to $150,000. More than half of the companies reporting corporate assistance made cash disbursements, which amounted to 40% of all corporate assistance expenditures.

The median for donations of product and property also rose significantly, from $28,000 to $100,000. About 25% of the respondents reported such donations, which also accounted for about one-quarter of all corporate assistance. The only category in which the median expenditure was lower in 1987 was the administrative cost for the contributions function, which fell to just under $100,000 compared to over $135,000 in 1986. As a percentage of the charitable contributions budget, median administrative costs continued to hover between 4% and 5% of contributions (see Table 8).

Table 1: Actual and Anticipated Changes in Contributions Budgets, 1986-1988
by Industry

Industry Classification	Number of Companies	1986-1987 Actual Percentage Change	1987-1988 Anticipated Percentage Change
Chemicals	20	3%	4%
Electrical machinery and equipment	17	35%a	−23%a
Food, beverage and tobacco	14	−13%	− 3%
Machinery, nonelectrical	10	−11	19
Paper and like products	6	22	− 4
Petroleum and gas[1]	21	−11	0
Pharmaceuticals	9	9	12
Other manufacturing[2]	12	− 8	2
Printing and publishing	6 a	−37%	14
Textiles and apparel	3	*	*
Transportation equipment[3]	7	− 4	12
Total: Manufacturing	125	4%	− 4%
Banking	20	3	2
Business services[4]	4	*	*
Finance	2	*	*
Insurance	22	2%	−15%
Retail and wholesale trade	5	1	0
Telecommunications	8	22	6
Transportation	2	*	*
Utilities	31	0	− 2
Total: Nonmanufacturing	94	9%	− 1%
Total: All Companies	219	5%	− 4%

*Total include all cases, but details omit industries with fewer than 5 cases.
aThese large changes reflect the effects of extraordinary noncash contributions.
[1]Includes mining companies.
[2]Includes primary metal industries, fabricated metal products, and stone, clay and glass products.
[3]Includes tire manufacturers.
[4]Includes engineering and construction companies.

Table 2: Anticipated Changes in Contributions Budget, 1988
By Size of Program

Program Size	Number of Companies	Median Percentage Increase 1987-1988	Aggregate Percentage Increase 1987-1988
Less than $500,000	66	2.7%	4.2%
$500,000 to $999,999	57	6.0	7.3
$1 million to $499,999	105	6.3	6.0
$5 million and over	72	2.6	−6.5
Total	300	4.5%	−3.6%

Table 3: Cash and Noncash Charitable Contributions of 75 Largest Donors, 1987

Company Rank	Total Contributions (dollars)	Cash	Cash as % Of Total	Securities	Securities as % Of Total	Company Product	Company Product as % Of Total	Property & Equipment	Property & Equipment as % Of Total
1	$136,415,202	$42,469,361	31%	$0	0%	$ 4,339,105	3%	$89,606,736	66%
2	98,327,500	76,232,900	78	0	0	19,080,400	19	3,014,200	3
3	57,286,000	37,645,000	66	0	0	0	0	19,641,000	34
4	49,749,899	36,601,777	74	0	0	13,148,122	26	0	0
5	39,647,698	39,647,698	100	0	0	0	0	0	0
6	38,173,878	29,302,088	77	0	0	8,553,052/	22	318,738	1
7	36,533,000	18,663,000	51	0	0	7,870,000	22	10,000,000	27
8	31,285,777	12,491,852	40	0	0	0	0	18,793,925	60
9	26,568,260	26,568,260	100	0	0	0	0	0	0
10	26,346,395	6,250,124	24	0	0	20,096,271	76	0	0
11	24,256,155	4,892,974	20	0	0	19,363,181	80	0	0
12	24,249,478	23,662,577	98	0	0	485,306	2	101,595	0
13	22,608,681	10,338,892	46	0	0	12,269,789	54	0	0
14	22,194,791	18,462,950	83	0	0	1,927,299	9	1,804,542	8
15	21,820,300	21,820,300	100	0	0	0	0	0	0
16	21,464,000	14,028,000	65	0	0	7,436,000	35	0	0
17	21,410,863	21,080,113	98	0	0	0	0	330,750	2
18	20,156,147	18,884,229	94	0	0	0	0	1,271,918	6
19	19,380,510	19,380,510	100	0	0	0	0	0	0
20	18,741,141	18,741,141	100	0	0	0	0	0	0
21	18,464,543	18,464,543	100	0	0	0	0	0	0
22	17,146,687	10,146,687	59	0	0	0	0	0	41
23	16,561,377	16,561,377	100	0	0	0	0	0	0
24	16,552,000	16,552,000	100	0	0	0	0	0	0
25	15,100,000	15,100,000	100	0	0	0	0	0	0
26	14,856,544	9,847,694	66	0	0	5,008,850	34	0	0
27	14,791,560	14,586,199	99	0	0	205,361	1	0	0
28	14,000,000	14,000,000	100	0	0	0	0	0	0
29	13,542,912	13,542,912	100	0	0	0	0	0	0
30	13,141,794	9,641,794	73	0	0	3,500,000	27	0	0
31	12,375,252	4,393,268	36	0	0	7,501,888	61	480,096	4
32	12,148,000	12,148,000	100	0	0	0	0	0	0
33	12,048,677	2,661,120	22	0	0	9,387,557	78	0	0
34	11,811,000	11,811,000	100	0	0	0	0	0	0
35	11,795,249	11,533,095	98	0	0	155,156	1	106,998	1
36	11,269,558	11,262,648	100	0	0	0	0	6,910	*
37	10,884,188	10,884,188	100	0	0	0	0	0	0
38	10,666,140	10,666,140	100	0	0	0	0	0	0
39	10,643,447	10,643,447	100	0	0	0	0	0	0
40	10,433,638	10,433,638	100	0	0	0	0	0	0
41	10,368,225	10,276,355	99	0	0	0	0	91,870	1
42	10,362,512	7,116,880	69	0	0	3,210,738	31	34,894	*
43	10,319,559	10,319,559	100	0	0	0	0	0	0
44	10,120,000	8,369,000	83	0	0	1,751,000	17	0	0
45	10,119,589	7,700,000	76	0	0	1,800,000	18	619,589	6
46	9,961,737	2,546,737	26	0	0	0	0	7,415,000	74
47	9,660,201	1,274,201	13	0	0	8,386,000	87	0	0
48	9,504,819	9,504,819	100	0	0	0	0	0	0
49	9,410,503	9,410,503	100	0	0	0	0	0	0
50	9,288,959	9,288,959	100	0	0	0	0	0	0

Total in a row may not add to 100 due to rounding.

*Less than 1 percent.

Table 3: Cash and Noncash Charitable Contributions of 75 Largest Donors, 1987 (continued)

Company Rank	Total Contributions (dollars)	Cash	Cash as % Of Total	Securities	Securities as % Of Total	Company Product	Company Product as % Of Total	Property & Equipment	Property & Equipment as % Of Total
51	9,213,670	7,939,577	86	0	0	1,274,093	14	0	0
52	9,062,725	9,062,725	100	0	0	0	0	0	0
53	9,033,495	8,426,891	93	0	0	606,604	7	0	0
54	8,900,000	8,900,000	100	0	0	0	0	0	0
55	8,415,214	8,415,214	100	0	0	0	0	0	0
56	8,411,591	2,411,591	29	0	0	5,700,000	68	300,000	4
57	8,369,443	8,215,112	98	0	0	0	0	154,331	2
58	8,267,635	8,267,635	100	0	0	0	0	0	0
59	8,099,883	8,099,883	100	0	0	0	0	0	0
60	8,063,854	8,063,854	100	0	0	0	0	0	0
61	7,828,684	7,828,684	100	0	0	0	0	0	0
62	7,700,000	7,700,000	100	0	0	0	0	0	0
63	7,496,118	7,496,118	100	0	0	0	0	0	0
64	7,404,991	3,324,840	45	0	0	4,080,151	0	0	0
65	7,305,421	7,305,421	100	0	0	0	0	0	0
66	7,060,000	6,600,000	93	0	0	0	0	460,000	7
67	6,906,164	6,906,164	100	0	0	0	0	0	0
68	6,747,240	6,747,240	100	0	0	0	0	0	0
69	6,690,176	4,905,353	73	0	0	1,693,301	250	91,522	1
70	6,658,064	6,658,064	100	0	0	0	0	0	0
71	6,539,939	6,539,939	100	0	0	0	0	0	0
72	6,532,000	6,532,000	100	0	0	0	0	0	0
73	6,529,986	6,529,986	100	0	0	0	0	0	0
74	6,116,672	6,116,672	100	0	0	0	0	0	0
75	5,944,839	5,798,015	98	0	0	146,824	0	0	0
Total	$1,313,262,149	$982,641,487	75%	0	0	$168,976,048	13%	$161,644,614	12%

Table 4: Cash and Noncash Giving, 1987—
Companies Grouped by Industry Classification (with at least 5 cases in each)[a]

Industry Classification	Number of Companies	Total Contributions Cash and Noncash ($ Thousands)	Cash as a Percent of Total Contributions	Securities as a Percent of Total Contributions	Company Product as a Percent of Total Contributions	Property and Equipment as a Percent of Total Contributions
Chemicals	25	$ 147,924	84%	0	9%	7%
Electrical machinery and equipment	23	373,398	55	0	19	27
Food, beverage and tobacco	18	174,161	72	0	28	*
Nonelectrical machinery	12	14,187	100	0	0	*
Paper and like products	12	30,065	72	0	1	27
Petroleum and gas[1]	21	202,426	98	0	1	1
Pharmaceuticals	11	96,678	74	0	26	*
Other manufacturing[2]	14	22,802	98	0	1	1
Printing and publishing	12	39,271	79	0	19	1
Textiles and apparel	5	3,407	97	0	3	0
Transportation equipment[3]	14	121,033	81	0	2	18
Total: Manufacturing	167	$1,225,352	75%	0	14%	12%
Banking	36	87,160	100	0	0	*
Business services[3]	8	14,095	87	13	*	*
Finance	8	19,774	100	0	*	0
Insurance	32	93,614	77	2	*	20
Retail and wholesale trade	8	54,144	100	0	*	0
Telecommunications	8	108,984	88	0	12	*
Transportation	5	4,466	98	0	2	0
Utilities	39	47,783	99	*	*	1
Total: Nonmanufacturing	144	430,019	91%	1%	3%	5%
Total: All Companies	311	$1,655,371	79%	*	11%	10%

[1]Includes mining companies.
[2]Includes primary metal industries, fabricated metal products, and stone, clay and glass products.
[3]Includes tire manufacturers.
[4]Includes engineering and construction companies.
*Less than 1 percent.
[a]Total may not add to 100 percent due to rounding.

Table 5: Comparison of Cash and Noncash Charitable Contributions, 1986 and 1987
243 Matched Companies

	1986 Total Contributions		1987 Total Contributions	
	Sum ($ Millions)	Percent	Sum ($ Millions)	Percent
Cash	$1,109.7	78.5%	$1,166.3	78.2
Securities...........................	2.5	0.2	4.1	0.3
Company product	181.5	12.8	166.5	11.2
Property and equipment	119.4	8.4	155.4	10.4
Total [a]	$1,413.1	100.0%	$1,492.2	100.0%

[a]Details may not add to totals due to rounding.

Table 6: Summary of Corporate Assistance Expenditures, 1987

Description	Number of Companies	Sum ($ Thousands)	Median
Cash Disbursements to 501(C) (3) Organizations			
Not Reported as Charitable Contributions	73	$ 74,343	$150,000
Loan of Company Personnel.............................	41	15,844	69,000
Donations of Product and Property Not			
Reported as Charitable Contributions......................	31	50,606	100,000
Use of Corporate Facilities or Services	38	13,193	42,123
Loans at Below-Market Yields.............................	15	6,009	100,000
Administrative Cost for Contributions Function	101	26,094	99,900
Total	136	$186,089	$193,747

Table 7: Corporate Assistance Expenditures, 1987
Companies Grouped by Industry Classification (with at least 5 cases in each)

		Sums		Medians	
Industry Classification	Number of Companies	Total Corporate Assistance	Corporate Assistance as Percent of Total Contributions	Total Corporate Assistance	Corporate Assistance as Percent of Total Contributions
Chemicals	12	$ 14,973	24%	$434,775	12%
Electrical machinery and equipment	8	34,103	12	612,346	5
Food, beverage and tobacco	13	59,793	42	550,000	7
Machinery, nonelectrical	6	2,222	30	76,792	6
Paper and like products	4	2,092	*	*	*
Petroleum and gas[1]	9	9,176	9	700,000	11
Pharmaceuticals	6	8,322	16	296,711	5
Other manufacturing[2]	3	1,696	*	*	*
Printing and publishing	4	3,860	*	*	*
Textiles and apparel	2	655	*	*	*
Transportation equipment[3]	2	5,639	*	*	*
Total: Manufacturing	69	$142,530	20%	$404,620	9%
Banking	15	7,746	25	251,192	22
Business services[4]	4	932	*	*	*
Finance	4	279	*	*	*
Insurance	22	12,765	16	125,162	13
Retail and wholesale trade	1	1,389	*	*	*
Telecommunications	2	9,307	*	*	*
Transportation	3	170	*	*	*
Utilities	16	10,970	45	76,500	7
Total: Nonmanufacturing	67	$ 43,559	25%	$125,071	12%
Total: All Companies	136	$186,089	21%	$193,747	12%

[1]Includes mining companies.
[2]Includes primary metal industries, fabricated metal products, and stone, clay and glass product.
[3]Includes tire manufacturers.
[4]Includes engineering and construction companies.
*Totals include all cases, but details omit industries with fewer than 5 cases.

Table 8: Administrative Cost as a Percent of Contributions Budget
Medians by Size of Contributions Budget

Size of Contributions Budget	Number of Companies	Administrative Cost as a Percent of Contributions Budget (Median)
Under $500,000	15	5.2%
$500,000—$1 million	14	4.5
$1 million—$5 million	45	5.4
Over $5 million	27	3.1
Total	101	4.5%

Median Value of Administrative Costs: $99,000

Chapter 2
Contributions Ratios: Guidelines for Decision Making

One of the most useful measures of contributions activity is the ratio of contributions to pretax income. This chapter and Appendix Tables 2 through 13 cover the various ways contributions managers can compare their company's contributions program to programs in peer companies.

In 1987, 328 companies from 18 different industry categories responded to The Conference Board Survey of Corporate Contributions. They reported a total of $1.6 billion in charitable contributions. Programs ranged in size from $100,000 to over $136 million, with a median contributions budget of $1.5 million.

Foundation Giving

It is unfortunate to report that despite a growing popularity for establishing corporate foundations for disbursing charitable contributions, donations from those foundations have steadily declined. Some industries, especially those in the service sector, have led the others in the use of corporate foundations as the vehicle for their giving. As of 1987, more than six out of ten surveyed companies reported having corporate foundations, compared to four out of ten a decade earlier (see Table 9). Conversely, the percentage of total charitable giving disbursed by corporate foundations has been dropping since 1982, when it reached a high of 42 percent. In 1987, only 36% of corporate contributions came from corporate foundations, continuing the downward trend.

Although 213 companies (65% of respondents) reported that they had a foundation, not all of them made grants in 1987. A total of 196 foundations disbursed $610 million; 13 of those foundations were their company's only source of charitable giving. Foundation grants ranged from $17,000 to $30 million, with a median of $1.3 million—a 36% increase over the 1986 median. The median contribution by direct giving programs, however, was down, from $780,000 in 1986 to $768,000 in 1987. The median size of foundation giving has consistently been substantially higher than that of direct giving programs.

The gap between the amount corporate foundations disburse in a given year and what they receive from their parent corporations widened once again in 1987, when corporate foundations gave out 25% more than they took in. [See Chart 9 for a graphic representation of the historical relationship between what foundations receive (pay-ins) and what they disburse (pay-outs).] There were some substantial grants to foundations by parent corporations in 1987—12 companies gave $10 million or more, with 9 of those grants intended to fund the foundation corpus. However, in the aggregate, corporate funding of the foundations fell short of foundation disbursements.

Industry Patterns

Historically, corporate contributions leaders—in terms of budget size and ratio of contributions to pretax income—have come from the manufacturing sector, and 1987 was no exception. The median contributions program among manufacturing firms in 1987 was $2.6 million, three times the size of the median for service companies ($853,000); and the median ratio of contributions to domestic pretax income was 1.41% for manufacturers, double the median ratio of .71% for service firms.

On the whole, contributions ratios were down in 1987, as profits increased—dramatically in some cases—but contributions budgets did not keep pace with the profit advances. For all companies, the median ratio of contributions to domestic pretax income declined from 1.17% to 1.05%, and the worldwide ratio fell from 1.01% to .85 percent. Among manufacturers in the matched sample, profits grew 20% between 1986 and 1987, but contributions budgets gained just 4%. However, matched service company contributions grew 9% despite a 20% drop in profits. (See Chart 10 for changes in worldwide pretax income and contributions by industry.)

Measures of industry leadership such as ratios and budget size (see adjacent box) continued to be dominated by industries with the largest firms, and particularly by industries with high proportions of noncash contributions (see Chapter 1).

Terms and Concepts Used in This Report

Two major formats for reporting contributions are used throughout this report. The first is a ratio, with contributions divided by such characteristics as pretax income and number of employees. The second is a percentage distribution, with contributions dollars apportioned among major beneficiary groups such as health and human services, education, culture and art, civic and community. In order to interpret these data correctly, it is important to understand the following:

Worldwide and "U.S.-Only" Data

Respondents to the questionnaire were asked to provide both worldwide and "U.S.-only" data on sales, assets, income before taxes, and number of employees. The worldwide data are the figures reported by corporations in their consolidated financial statements. The "U.S.-only" financial data reflect sales, assets and pretax income derived solely from U.S. operations. The employee-size data reflect only those workers employed in the United States. For those companies that are not multinational, "worldwide" and "U.S.-only" data are identical.

While the worldwide data are consistent with tabulated statistics on the corporate sector as reported by various U.S. government agencies, it should be noted that there are no comparable "U.S.-only" figures. U.S. data have customarily been included in this series of Conference Board reports, however, in order to facilitate comparison with the contributions figures, which reflect giving only to domestic or U.S.-based beneficiaries. (Overseas giving is discussed on page 18.)

Contributions

Corporate contributions and gifts reported to the IRS normally include gifts of property as well as gifts of cash, and the survey questionnaire specifically asked respondents to include the dollar value of gifts of property reported as contributions on the company's income tax return. However, there are two major differences between the contributions figures derived from Internal Revenue Service (IRS) sources and those reported in this study. While both sets of figures include direct giving by corporations, the first difference lies in the treatment of dollars going *into* and *out of* corporate foundations within a given year.

The IRS figures reflect dollars given by a corporation to its foundation, while the survey figures reflect dollars donated by corporate foundations to eligible beneficiaries. This is in keeping with study objectives to measure the flow of dollars actually reaching beneficiaries in any calendar year. Dollars given to the foundation are not necessarily expended within the same year.

The second major difference between the IRS and the survey figures is the fact that the IRS data reflect the total universe of approximately two million corporations that file tax returns, while the survey data are compiled from a sample of these firms that is weighted toward larger companies.

Corporate Assistance

Corporate-assistance expenditures are six categories of items that are given to assist social, charitable or other groups to promote the well-being of society, but are *not* taken as a charitable deduction by corporations. These include cash grants given to tax-exempt, 501 (c) (3) organizations that are not reported as contributions; loans of company personnel; donations of products, equipment and property charged to business expense; loans, deposits and investments for social purposes at below-market rates of return; loans of company facilities and services at no charge or below cost; and the direct costs the company incurs in administering the contributions function.

Corporate Social Expenditure

The sum of charitable contributions and corporate-assistance expenditures, appears only in Table 8B. It represents an attempt to estimate a total for social involvement by major corporations.

Ratios

It is common practice in the contributions field to speak both of the 5-percent limit on giving, and of setting a "5-percent" target. Since 1936, the Internal Revenue Code has allowed corporations to deduct contributions to charitable organizations up to a maximum of 5 percent of the corporation's *taxable* income with a five-year carry forward. Under the Economic Recovery Tax Act of 1981, this limit was raised to 10 percent. Because taxable income is a closely held figure, it is not possible to collect it from corporations for use in this report. Instead, the ratio is calculated on pretax income.

Major Categories of Organizations

The problem of classifying and defining the five major areas of corporate support and their subcategories is a continuing one. Classification is made on the basis of the major program objective or organizational goal of the *donee* group. The five major categories of organization used in this survey—health and human services, education, culture and the arts, civic and community, and "other"—include all grant formats: matching gifts, operating support, program support, and capital support. (For more detail on categories, see box on page 14.)

Companies with Losses in 1987

In 1987, 24 companies (7%) participating in the survey experienced worldwide income losses. One-third of the firms were banks, and one-sixth were petroleum and gas companies. The remaining firms were widely distributed over both the manufacturing and service sectors.

Charitable contributions from these firms totaled nearly $81 million, with 15 of the 24 giving over $1 million each. Six of the companies appear on the list of the top 75 donors. The median contributions budget among these loss companies was $1.7 million—higher than the median for companies with positive pretax income.

Foundations did not have a substantial role in maintaining charitable giving levels for these loss companies in 1987. Half of the companies reporting losses have corporate foundations, but the foundations accounted for only one-quarter of the donations made by these companies. The foundations disbursed approximately $10 million more than they took in from the parent corporations.

Major Donors

More than three-quarters of the contributions reported in The Conference Board Survey come from less than one-quarter of the survey respondents. The companies listed in Appendix Table 8A, the "75 Largest Donors," gave a total of $1.3 billion in 1987. The top-ranked company gave $136 million, a five-fold increase compared to the amount contributed by the top-ranked company a decade ago. The median contribution for the 1987 top-ranked companies was $10.6 million, approximately the same as in 1986. However, contributions to pretax-income ratios were considerably low-

Industry Leaders

Median Contributions as a Percent of U.S. Pretax Income

Other manufacturing	2.66%
Food, beverage, and tobacco	2.06
Electrical machinery and equipment	1.71
Pharmaceuticals	1.67
Machinery, nonelectrical	1.42

Median Total Contributions ($ Thousands)

Petroleum and gas	$10,320
Pharmaceuticals	9,532
Telecommunications	8,431
Food, beverage, and tobacco	5,943
Printing and publishing	3,746

Aggregate Total Contributions ($ Thousands)

Electrical machinery and equipment	$359,587
Food, beverage, and tobacco	$158,383
Petroleum and gas	$140,143
Chemicals	$129,875
Pharmaceuticals	$ 87,397

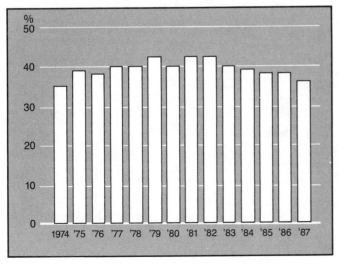

Chart 8:
Percent of Total Corporate Contributions Provided by Corporate Foundations

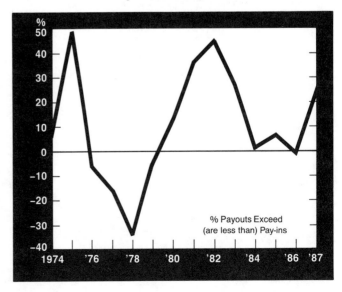

Chart 9:
Relationship of Foundation Payouts to Pay-ins

er in 1987 among the top 75. The median ratio was 1.68%, compared to 2.2% in 1986. Only five companies on the list gave over 5%; over one-third of the companies gave more than 2% of U.S. pretax income in charitable contributions.

The largest contributions budgets grew twice as fast as those of survey respondents in the aggregate. A comparison of 1986 and 1987 contributions levels for the companies on the list of the top 75 donors showed an overall increase of 10%, compared to the 5% gain posted by all companies in the survey. However, of the $110 million increase reported by the top 75 companies, over $100 million was from a *single* company, and most of that was the result an extraordinary

gift of property. Noncash contributions also played an important role in the substantial hikes reported by other companies on the list of leading donors.

In addition to the top-ranked company, eight other companies raised their contributions levels in 1987 by 35% or more, in dollar amounts ranging from $3 million to $15 million. Of those, only two were entirely cash increases, and they were relatively new programs. The remainder enlarged their contributions programs through product and/or property donations. Among the top 75 companies, noncash contributions accounted for 28% of all giving, compared to 21% for all survey respondents. (See Table 3 in Chapter 1 for a

Chart 10:
Percentage Change in Contributions and Worldwide Pretax Income, 1986 and 1987, by Industry

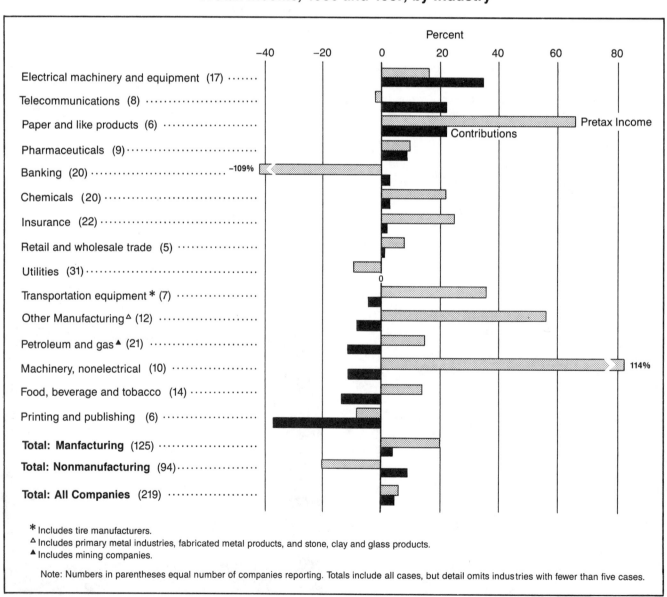

* Includes tire manufacturers.
△ Includes primary metal industries, fabricated metal products, and stone, clay and glass products.
▲ Includes mining companies.

Note: Numbers in parentheses equal number of companies reporting. Totals include all cases, but detail omits industries with fewer than five cases.

detailed breakdown of the cash and noncash components of the top 75 donors.)

1987 Ratios: Quartiles for Key Groups

Comparison with peer groups is one step in the process for determining contribution budget levels. A basic tool of comparison for contributions managers is the ratio of contributions to pretax income. Appendix Tables 9A through 13B present the range of contributions to pretax-income ratios via the 25th, 50th, and 75th percentiles. Survey respondents are grouped by size of program, income, industry, assets, and sales.

When companies are grouped by the size of their contributions programs, as in Appendix Tables 9A and 9B, a straightforward pattern emerges: As the size of the contributions program increases, ratios also increase. Medians in all size categories in 1987 were down from 1986 levels, in amounts ranging from 9% to 23 percent.

Appendix Tables 10A and 10B group companies by size of income. In general, the pattern is the inverse of ratios grouped by program size; as income rises, contributions ratios fall. However, the pattern holds only at the low end of the table, for companies with incomes under $250 million. The smallest companies have considerably higher ratios, and also a much broader range between the 25th and 75th percentiles, than do larger companies. Above $250 million in income, however, ratios begin to climb again. Many of the companies in these higher income ranges are also the companies with the largest contributions budgets, so the higher contributions levels tend to push the ratios up.

Over the years, contributions ratios grouped by the size of company assets, in Appendix Tables 12A and 12B, have not shown any particularly consistent pattern in the relationship of asset size to contributions to income ratios. Median ratios tend to be highest for companies in the lowest asset ranges, slightly lower for companies in the highest asset ranges, and the lowest in the middle ranges. However, domestic ratios in 1987 grouped by assets had an erratic pattern, with some ratios considerably higher than 1986 levels, and others much lower, with no apparent underlying cause.

Contributions ratios grouped according to sales, Appendix Tables 13A and 13B, follow a similar pattern to ratios grouped by income, with higher ratios at the lower end of the ranges.

Contributions per Employee

Some companies use the number of employees as well as pretax income as a guideline in determining contributions levels. In 1987, the first time since 1981 when The Conference Board first began to report it, the median contributions per employee fell, from $164 to $157 (see Chart 12). Among firms of different sizes, however, the pattern was mixed. The smallest companies, with under 1,000 employees, continued to have a substantially higher median than any other category, and the median grew slightly over its 1986 level. (See Chart 13.) However, medians fell in three categories: 2,500-4,999 (down 32%); 5,000-9,999 (down 13%); and 15,000-24,999 (down 5%). The largest companies, on the other hand, had higher median contributions per employee in 1987: 25,000-49,999 (up 26%); and over 50,000 (up 22%).

Chart 11:
Percentage Change in Contributions and Worldwide Pretax Income, 1977 to 1987

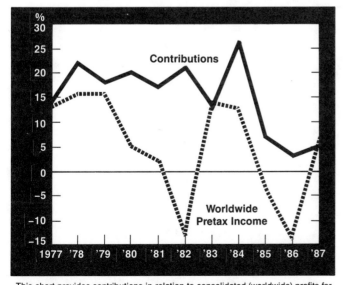

This chart provides contributions in relation to consolidated (worldwide) profits for matched-case companies participating in consecutive survey years.

Chart 12:
Median Contributions per Employee 1982 to 1987

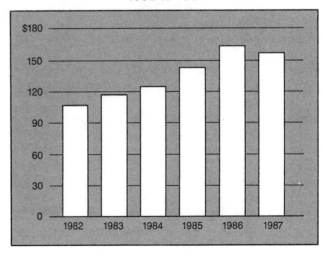

Chart 13:
Contributions per U.S. Employee, 1987
Medians

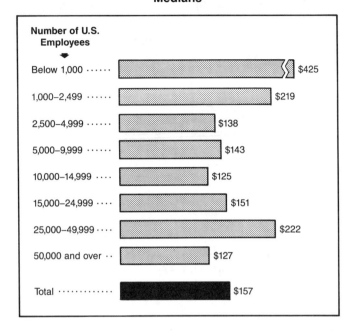

Number of U.S. Employees	
Below 1,000	$425
1,000–2,499	$219
2,500–4,999	$138
5,000–9,999	$143
10,000–14,999	$125
15,000–24,999	$151
25,000–49,999	$222
50,000 and over	$127
Total	$157

Overseas Giving

Many survey respondents with foreign operations make contributions overseas in addition to their domestic giving. In 1987, about one-quarter (78) of the survey participants reported such overseas contributions. Overseas giving totalled $110 million, down about 3% from 1986 levels. Contributions ranged from less than $1,000 to $49 million, with a median of $162,000. In the aggregate, overseas giving accounted for about 12% of the domestic contributions made by these companies, with a median of 4 percent.

Overseas donations on a large scale are mainly made by large, multinational firms with facilities in the countries where they make their contributions. Most of the overseas contributions reported in the survey are made by companies in the electrical machinery and equipment industry ($56 million) and the petroleum and gas industry ($23 million). A number of other industries reported foreign contributions of over $5 million: pharmaceuticals ($8 million); chemicals ($7 million); banking ($6 million); and transportation equipment ($5 million).

Table 9: Concentration of Foundations, by Industry
Companies Grouped by Industry Class

Industry Classification	Number of Companies	Number of Foundations	Percent of Companies with Foundations
Chemicals	26	18	69%
Electrical machinery and equipment	24	17	71
Food, beverage and tobacco	20	16	80
Machinery, nonelectrical	13	9	69
Paper and like products	13	10	77
Petroleum and gas[1]	22	15	68
Pharmaceuticals	11	10	91
Other manufacturing[2]	16	14	88
Printing and publishing	13	7	54
Textiles and apparel	5	4	80
Transportation equipment[3]	16	13	81
Total: Manufacturing	179	133	74%
Banking	38	24	63
Business services[4]	8	4	50
Finance	8	7	88
Insurance	32	24	75
Retail and wholesale trade	8	5	63
Telecommunications	8	7	88
Transportation	5	3	60
Utilities	42	6	14
Total: Nonmanufacturing	149	80	54%
Total: All Companies	328	213	65%

[1]Includes mining companies.
[2]Includes primary metal industries, fabricated metal products, and stone, clay and glass products.
[3]Includes tire manufacturers.
[4]Includes engineering and construction companies.

Definitions of Terms

The Five Major Categories of Beneficiaries

Health and Human Services

Includes support for national health organizations (such as American Cancer Society, Salk Institute, National Homecaring Council, Memorial Sloan-Kettering Cancer Center); national human-services organizations (such as American Red Cross, National Council on Aging, National Committee for Prevention of Child Abuse, Planned Parenthood of America); national youth organizations, (such as Boys Clubs of America); federated drives such as the United Way; support for hospitals; local youth organizations (such as Boys Clubs, Boy and Girl Scouts, YMCA); and other local health and human-service agencies. Among other things, such organizations are concerned with safety, recreation, family planning, drug abuse, and disaster relief.

Education

Includes support for institutions of higher education, precollege educational institutions, state and local educational fund-raising groups, economic education groups, and education-related organizations. Program support for research projects funded from the contributions budget is included; however, support of contractual university research is generally excluded.

Educational programs such as employee tuition-refund plans are excluded when funded out of the personnel, public relations, or other expense budgets.

Culture and the Arts

Includes visual and performing arts organizations, libraries, museums, cultural centers, arts funds or councils, and the like. Includes support for public radio and television if funded from the contributions budget. Excludes any support funded from expense budgets.

Civic and Community

Includes support for national organizations in public-policy research (such as AEI, Brookings, CED); national community improvement (such as Neighborhood Housing Services, Opportunities Industrialization Centers, Local Initiatives Support Corporation, National Urban League, Center for Community Change); national environment and ecology (such as National Wildlife Fund, National Conservation Foundation, Sierra Club); national justice and law organizations (such as Institute for Civil Justice, National Council on Crime and Delinquency, Legal Defense and Education Funds: NOW, MALDEF, Mountain States); other national organizations (such as Independent Sector, National Executive Service Corps, Population Resource Center); municipal or statewide improvement (such as Governors' Task Forces, Planning Associations, Economic Development Council of NYC); local community improvement organizations (such as neighborhood or community-based groups, housing programs, economic development and employment such as PIC's. Job Training Programs); legal systems and services (such as Legal Aid Societies); local environment and ecology (such as zoos, parks, conservation activities); and other local civic and community organizations. Includes local projects such as transportation, housing, law and order, fire prevention, grants to local and state governments, and support of study groups to resolve social problems.

Other

Includes support for religious activities, U.S. groups whose principal objective is aid in other countries, (such as CARE, IESC, Council on Foreign Relations), and charitable support for special sports or patriotic events (such as Olympics, Statue of Liberty).

Chapter 3
Priorities in Corporate Giving

Over the long term, the distribution of corporate contributions among the major categories of nonprofit beneficiaries acts as something of a barometer of shifting corporate priorities. Corporate goals and emphases in contributions programs tend to be reflected in the amount of money corporations devote to individual categories. In any single year, however, the percentage of total contributions directed to a particular category may be unusually inflated or deflated because of extraordinary gifts. Although these gifts also convey a message about corporate choices, the broader view of several years is a more accurate picture of identifiable trends in corporate giving. Such an extraordinary gift was made in 1987, which sharply altered how the "pie" of corporate contributions was cut, but which is not expected to be a signal of a major shift in where corporate giving is headed.

Extraordinary giving aside, corporate giving is headed gradually away from health and human services causes, particulary federated campaigns such as United Way, and away from educational giving, after a brief surge in 1986, due mainly to a single large gift. There are also slight declines for cultural and arts beneficiaries. Some renewed strength is apparent in civic and community activities.

At 27%, the proportion of corporate contributions donated to health and human services reached its lowest point in 1987. Except for 1985, when the percentage edged up 1 point, the proportion of giving going to this category has been progressively declining. In ten years, the percentage has

Chart 14
Distribution of the Contributions Dollar, 1986 and 1987

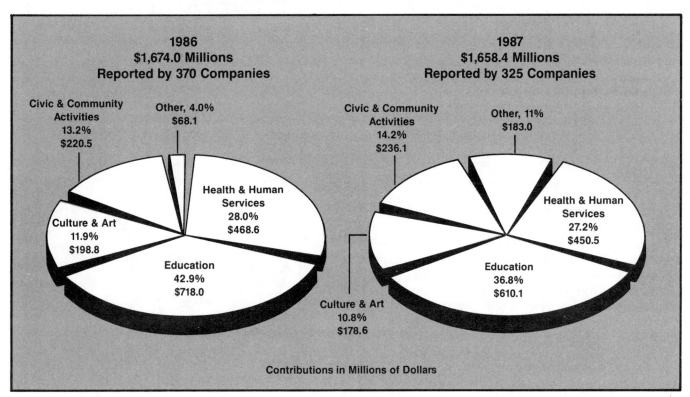

1986
$1,674.0 Millions
Reported by 370 Companies

Civic & Community Activities
13.2%
$220.5

Other, 4.0%
$68.1

Culture & Art
11.9%
$198.8

Health & Human Services
28.0%
$468.6

Education
42.9%
$718.0

1987
$1,658.4 Millions
Reported by 325 Companies

Civic & Community Activities
14.2%
$236.1

Other, 11%
$183.0

Culture & Art
10.8%
$178.6

Health & Human Services
27.2%
$450.5

Education
36.8%
$610.1

Contributions in Millions of Dollars

dropped ten points, from 37% in 1978. The major underlying cause of the loss of share has been the diminishing proportion of corporate contributions for federated campaigns. In 1987, federated campaigns received only 12% of total contributions, down from 13% in 1986, and 21% ten years ago.

Educational gifts totalled 37% of all contributions in 1987, a sharp drop of 6 percentage points from 1986. However, 1986 figures included an extraordinary gift of property to a university; this gift skewed the proportion earmarked for educational causes. Except for 1982 and 1986, when giving to education reached 41% and 43% respectively, over the last ten years education has represented between 37% and 39% of total contributions. So, while the change between 1986 and 1987 levels appears quite severe, the 1987 percentage is actually within the normal range for giving to education, although at the low end of the range. (See Chart 15.)

The proportion of giving to cultural and arts programs dropped slightly to approximately 11 percent. Over the last ten years, giving to this category has been quite stable, ranging between 10% and 12% of total contributions.

Civic and community activities garnered an additional percentage point of total contributions in 1987, up from 13% to 14 percent. As they have over the last five years, property donations once again played a role in raising the proportion of giving received by beneficiaries in this category.

An unusually large proportion of corporate contributions—11%—went to the category of "other" organizations in 1987, largely because of an extraordinary gift of property. The $90 million gift, plus an additional $10 million in cash, was donated to an organization that the donor company considered an exception to the four major contribution categories. The $100 million gift accounted for more than half of the $183 million given to "other" beneficiaries by all surveyed respondents.

Health and Human Services

Although the proportion of total contributions accounted for by health and human services was lower in 1987 than in 1986, aggregate dollars to health and human services did grow. Matched-sample companies gave $13 million more to health and human services beneficiaries in 1987, an aggregate increase of approximately 4 percent. The median dollar size of giving to this category also rose among matched-sample companies, from $562,000 to $599,000.

Among all survey respondents, the median contribution to health and human services was $538,000, and the median percentage of total contributions was 37 percent.

Although giving to health and human services organizations is not a high priority among companies with very large contributions budgets (see box, "The Relationship of Program Size to Priorities"), a few of the companies on the list of the top 75 donors gave extraordinarily high portions of their budgets to health and human services. (See Chapter Table 10.) Five companies with total contributions of $6 mil-

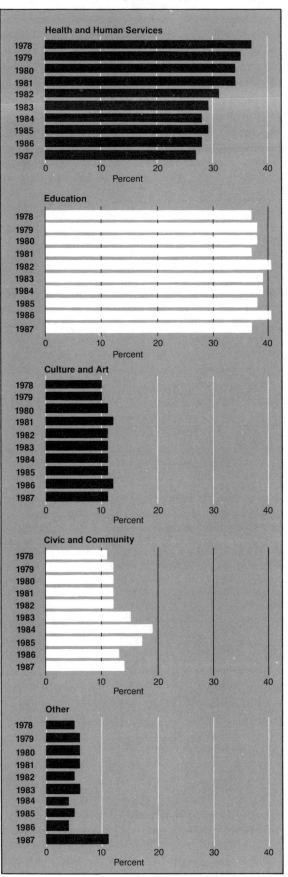

Chart 15:
Beneficiaries of Corporate Support, 1978–1987

Historically, two strong patterns have emerged in corporate giving that are related to the size of the contributions budget: (1) the smaller the budget, the greater the proportion to health and human services; and (2) the larger the budget, the greater the portion to education.

In general, smaller budgets tend to mean fewer resources of all types—staff, time, and so forth. Without those resources, the individual responsible for contributions decisions may find it extremely difficult either to thoroughly assess community needs or to conduct a rigorous screening process of grant requests. In such situations, it has been more effective to delegate those functions to the United Way or other federated giving programs.

The predominance of educational giving among companies with the largest programs (over $5 million) reflects the industrial composition of this size category. Most of the companies with substantial contributions budgets are in the manufacturing sector—particularly transportation equipment manufacturers, petroleum and gas companies, pharmaceutical companies, and electrical equipment and machinery manufacturers. These industries have a history of major funding of educational programs—especially higher education—because of their critical need for highly trained technical staff.

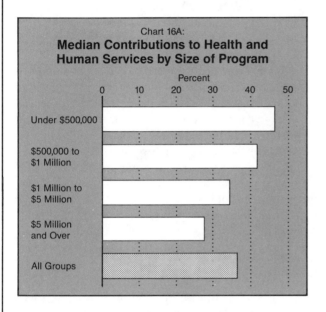

Chart 16A:
Median Contributions to Health and Human Services by Size of Program

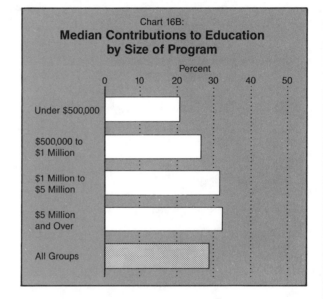

Chart 16B:
Median Contributions to Education by Size of Program

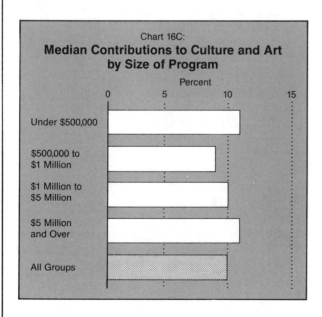

Chart 16C:
Median Contributions to Culture and Art by Size of Program

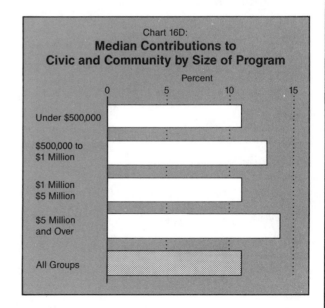

Chart 16D:
Median Contributions to Civic and Community by Size of Program

lion or more gave between 50% and 92% to health and human services. All but one of them were food companies, which make sizable product donations to food clearinghouses, such as Second Harvest.

Other Health and Human Services Organizations

There was a slight shift in the distribution of giving within the category of health and human services in 1987. (See Chart 19.) Giving to hospitals and matching gifts maintained stable proportions, but all other nonfederated health and human services organizations (specified and unspecified combined) accounted for 47% of total giving to the

---

The Top Five Industry Leaders in Giving to Health and Human Services

Aggregate Percent of Total Contributions

Utilities	46%
Food, beverage, and tobacco	46
Textiles and apparel	43
Transportation	41
Nonelectrical machinery	40

Median Percent of Total Contributions

Transportation	54%
Utilities	52
Banking	46
Nonelectrical machinery	43
Insurance	42

Aggregate Dollar Value of Contributions ($ Millions)

Food, beverage, and tobacco	$80
Electrical machinery and equipment	$55
Petroleum and gas	$44
Chemicals	$38
Transportation equipment	$31

Median Dollar Value of Contributions ($ Thousands)

Petroleum and gas	$2,467
Food, beverage, and tobacco	$2,249
Telecommunications	$2,185
Pharmaceuticals	$1,830
Other manufacturing	$1,709

---

category. The increase of 3 percentage points was at the expense of federated campaigns.

Corporate giving to hospitals has slowed considerably over the last decade—from 4% to 2% of total contributions. Our survey respondents reported contributions of $31 million for 1987, but this was about the same dollar figure reported in 1978.

Federated Campaigns

Although federated campaigns continued to diminish in importance as part of our respondent companies total contributions programs, the corporate donation to United Way remained the largest single item in many companies' budgets. The median contribution to federated campaigns climbed over 20% to $293,000 in 1987, although aggregate contributions rose only about 1 percent. (See Table 11 for median donations to federated campaigns grouped by program size.)

Giving to federated campaigns is stronger among companies in the service sector. Nonmanufacturing companies gave an aggregate 17% of total contributions to federated campaigns, compared to only 11% from manufacturers. (See Chart 17.) The difference is particularly pronounced when measured by dollars per employee to federated campaigns (Chart 18). Service sector companies gave a median of $41 per employee, while manufacturing firms gave $21. Companies with small contributions programs, or companies with high visibility in local markets, such as banks, utilities, and retailers, tend to place more emphasis on giving to federated campaigns.

Education

In the redistribution of contributions among beneficiaries in 1987, education recipients got considerably less than they had in 1986. Among the matched-sample companies, total giving to education dropped $70 million—nearly 12%—the largest decrease among the five categories. Part of the drop can be explained by a $40 million gift of property in 1986 that temporarily elevated total giving to education. But the decrease was not only in aggregate dollars. The median contribution to educational organizations also fell, from $522,000 in 1986 to $470,000 in 1987. However, the median percentage change in giving to education was an increase of two percent.

Educational giving continued as a major priority for manufacturing firms, which gave a median of 37% of total contributions to educational causes, compared to 22% for service companies. (See Appendix Table 17 for quartiles by individual industries.) The median dollar value of contributions to education by manufacturers was $844,000, over three times the size of the median service donation of $245,000.

Higher Education

Twenty-six percent of all corporate contributions went to higher education (including scholarships and fellowships and matching gifts) in 1987. Over the last ten years, the percentage has ranged between 26% and 29%, except for 1986, when it reached more than 32% because of a large property gift. Industries that place a high priority on giving to higher education tend to depend upon a highly trained workforce of engineers and scientists. They include electrical machinery and equipment (34% to higher education); petroleum and gas (33%); telecommunications (33%); and chemical companies (30%). Business services firms also reported major contributions (40%). The median dollar value of gifts to higher education was $191,000, the second highest subcategory after federated campaigns.

A sizable part of many companies' contributions programs is employee matching gifts. Matching gifts to education reached over $108 million in 1987, a nearly four-fold increase from ten years before. As a proportion of total contributions, matching gifts to education have also grown, from nearly

The Top Five Industry Leaders in Giving to Education

Aggregate Percent of Total Contributions

Transportation equipment	54%
Petroleum and gas	45
Telecommunications	45
Business services	43
Chemicals	42

Median Percent of Total Contributions

Electrical machinery and equipment	48%
Petroleum and gas	44
Chemicals	40
Transportation equipment	38
Textiles and apparel	37

Aggregate Dollar Value of Contributions ($ Millions)

Electrical machinery and equipment	$154
Petroleum and gas	$ 91
Transportation equipment	$ 68
Chemicals	$ 57
Telecommunications	$ 49

Median Dollar Value of Contributions ($ Thousands)

Chemicals	$4,199
Pharmaceuticals	$2,899
Electrical machinery and equipment	$2,353
Petroleum and gas	$2,216
Telecommunications	$2,136

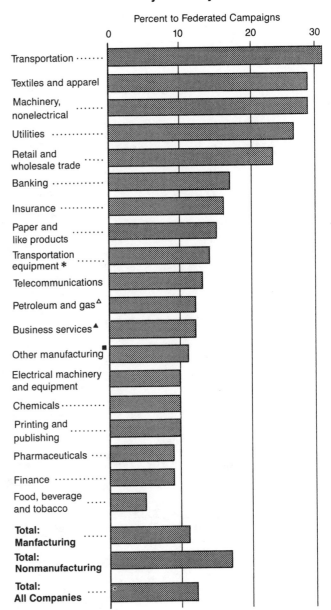

Chart 17:
Contributions to Federated Campaigns as a Percentage of Total Giving By Industry

Percent to Federated Campaigns

* Includes tire manufacturers.
△ Includes mining companies.
▲ Includes engineering and construction companies.
■ Includes primary metal industries, fabricated metal products, and stone, clay and glass products.

4% in 1978 to 6.5% in 1987. Industries with high proportions of matching gifts to education are finance (13%); petroleum and gas (12%); and business services (12%). The median dollar value of matching gifts was $141,000, up from $121,000 in 1986.

Precollege Education

Contrary to expectations, corporate contributions to precollege education *lost* ground in 1987. Contributions in this category totaled only $25 million, compared to $40 million in 1986; and the proportion of total contributions dropped from 2.4% to 1.5 percent. Only the paper industry gave more than 3% in this category. The median gift was $25,000.

In 1987, the issue of corporate support for precollege education—particularly in the public schools—was widely discussed. Several corporations took leadership roles in calling the need for company support to the attention of their peers. Although much was said about what corporations could and should do, the results—i.e., the funds to provide the support—did not show up in The Conference Board survey. It is possible that some of the money donated to higher education is planned for teacher training programs or curriculum development projects that will ultimately affect the

Chart 18:
Contributions per Employee to Federated Campaigns, 1987

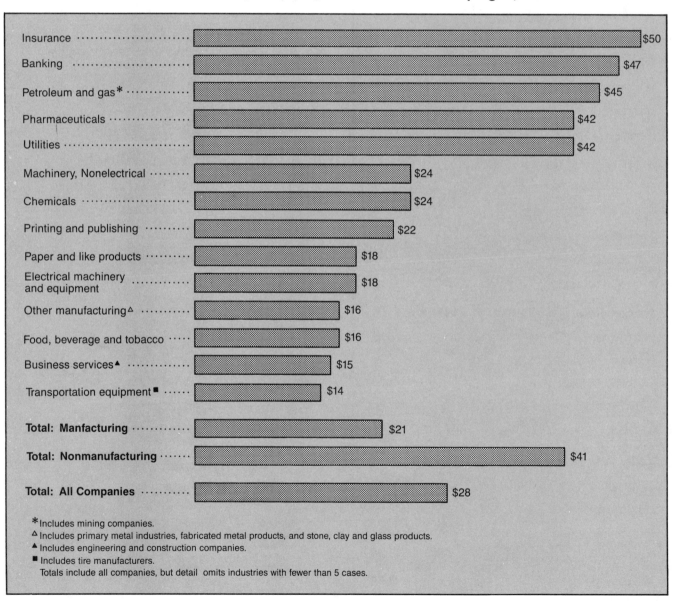

Insurance — $50
Banking — $47
Petroleum and gas* — $45
Pharmaceuticals — $42
Utilities — $42
Machinery, Nonelectrical — $24
Chemicals — $24
Printing and publishing — $22
Paper and like products — $18
Electrical machinery and equipment — $18
Other manufacturing△ — $16
Food, beverage and tobacco — $16
Business services▲ — $15
Transportation equipment■ — $14

Total: Manfacturing — $21
Total: Nonmanufacturing — $41

Total: All Companies — $28

*Includes mining companies.
△ Includes primary metal industries, fabricated metal products, and stone, clay and glass products.
▲ Includes engineering and construction companies.
■ Includes tire manufacturers.
Totals include all companies, but detail omits industries with fewer than 5 cases.

precollege population. But in general, the evidence from the survey indicates that corporations are *not* shifting money into the schools.

Culture and the Arts

Giving to cultural and arts organizations declined somewhat in 1987, both in aggregate dollars and in percentage of total contributions. Among the matched sample, total dollars declined about 5%, and the percentage dropped about 1 point, from 12% to 11 percent. The median dollar value

of contributions in this category also declined for the matched-case companies, from $153,000 to $134,000. Despite the declines, giving to the arts remained within the range it has held for the last ten years (between 10% and 12% of total contributions).

Cultural giving tends to be stronger among companies in the service sector, which overall gave over 15% of total contributions to the arts, compared to about 9% for manufacturers (See Chart 23.)

Matching gifts to cultural and arts groups were reported by about one-third of the respondents, with a median dollar value of $45,000. Matching gifts accounted for less than 1% of total contributions.

The Top Five Industry Leaders in Giving to Culture and the Arts

Aggregate Percent of Total Contributions

Transportation	24%
Other manufacturing	24
Retail and wholesale trade	22
Printing and publishing	21
Finance	17

Median Percent of Total Contributions

Telecommunications	19%
Printing and publishing	19
Transportation	19
Finance	17
Insurance	15

Aggregate Dollar Value of Contributions ($ Millions)

Electrical machinery and equipment	$27
Petroleum and gas	$24
Telecommunications	$18
Food, beverage, and tobacco	$16
Banking	$13

Median Dollar Value of Contributions ($ Thousands)

Telecommunications	$1,826
Petroleum and gas	$ 820
Printing and publishing	$ 458
Food, beverage, and tobacco	$ 299
Finance	$ 251

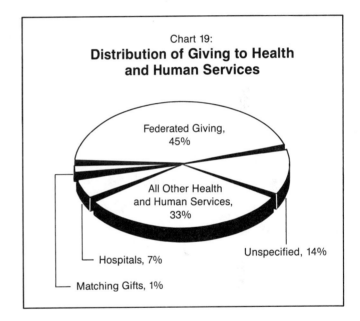

Chart 19:
Distribution of Giving to Health and Human Services

Federated Giving, 45%

All Other Health and Human Services, 33%

Hospitals, 7%

Matching Gifts, 1%

Unspecified, 14%

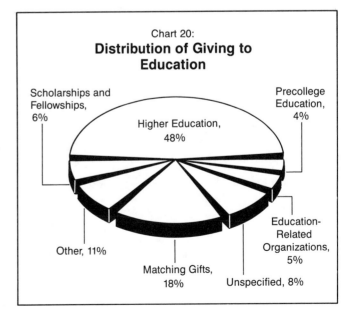

Chart 20:
Distribution of Giving to Education

Scholarships and Fellowships, 6%

Precollege Education, 4%

Higher Education, 48%

Other, 11%

Matching Gifts, 18%

Unspecified, 8%

Education-Related Organizations, 5%

Civic and Community Activities

Giving to civic and community activities advanced in 1987, mainly because of the impact of property gifts. Among the matched-sample companies total giving in this category grew almost 8%, with a median percentage increase of about 2 percent. The median dollar value of contributions rose from $154,000 in 1986 to $166,000 in 1987. Service companies reported an aggregate of 19% of total contributions to civic and community groups, compared to about 13% for manufacturers. One of the largest subcategories of civic and community activities is community improvement—economic development and community revitalization programs. In 1987, giving to these types of programs was down $20 million, from $73 million in 1986, even though the drop amounted to just a one percent fall in total contributions. However, there were a few industries that increased their donations to these types of programs: petroleum and gas (from 0.9% to 6%); business services (from 1.1% to nearly 5%); and insurance (from 1.1% to 4.5%). Contributions to housing were also down, to about $6 million—less than half of what it was when it peaked at over $14 million in 1984. Banking was the only industry to give more than 1% of its contributions to housing.

The Top Five Industry Leaders in Giving to Civic and Community Activities

Aggregate Percent of Total Contributions

Paper and like products	35%
Insurance	33
Finance	27
Retail and wholesale trade	20
Petroleum and gas	19

Median Percent of Total Contributions

Finance	20%
Petroleum and gas	15
Business services	15
Telecommunications	15
Retail and wholesale trade	14

Aggregate Dollar Value of Contributions ($ Millions)

Petroleum and gas	$39
Insurance	$31
Electrical equipment and machinery	$27
Chemicals	$25
Food, beverage, and tobacco	$20

Median Dollar Value of Contributions ($ Thousands)

Petroleum and gas	$1,305
Telecommunications	$1,103
Pharmaceuticals	$ 709
Food, beverage, and tobacco	$ 502
Transportation equipment	$ 295

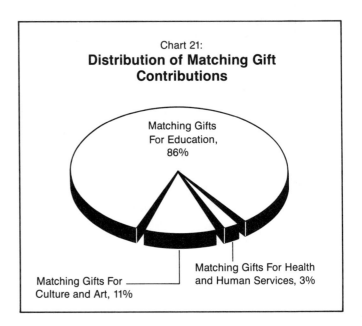

Chart 21:
Distribution of Matching Gift Contributions

Matching Gifts For Education, 86%

Matching Gifts For Culture and Art, 11%

Matching Gifts For Health and Human Services, 3%

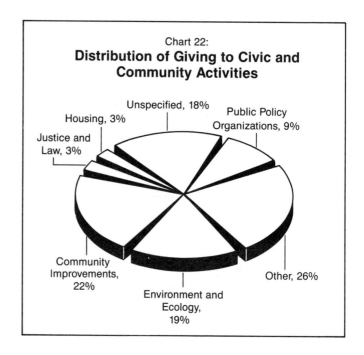

Chart 22:
Distribution of Giving to Civic and Community Activities

Unspecified, 18%
Housing, 3%
Justice and Law, 3%
Public Policy Organizations, 9%
Community Improvements, 22%
Environment and Ecology, 19%
Other, 26%

Giving to other civic and community organizations—charities concerned on the local level with transportation, housing, law and order, fire prevention, and so forth—grew strongly, from $35 million to $62 million, and from 2% to nearly 4% of total contributions.

Donations to public policy groups increased to $22 million, after several years at $15 million to $16 million; financial services companies gave nearly 10% of total contributions to this subcategory. Environmental and ecological organizations also advanced, from $36 million to $44 million. Three industries continued to make major contributions in this area: paper companies (23%); insurance companies (which donate property) (19%); and chemical companies (8%). For chemical and paper companies, the priority they give these organizations reflects the corporations' commitment to improve and replenish the environment.

"Other" Organizations

A $90 million gift of property pushed contributions to "other" organizations to a record high in 1987 of $183 million or 11% of total contributions. In the aggregate, contributions to this category grew 225% among matched-sample companies. Median figures, which aren't affected by the one extraordinary value, also indicated growth. The median dol-

lar value rose from $39,000 to $41,000. The median percentage change among matched companies was about 2 percent.

Not all of the growth recorded in this category is due to the previously mentioned property gift, however. Several industries reported higher-than-normal giving in this area. In some instances, the increases are meaningful, but in others this miscellaneous grouping may reflect grants that did not easily fit into the remaining categories. Pharmaceutical companies regularly donate large quantities of drugs to U.S.-based relief organizations, which distribute the drugs overseas, and the companies report these major donations in the "other" category. In 1987, pharmaceutical donations were consider-

---

The Top Five Industry Leaders in Giving to "Other" Groups

Aggregate Percent of Total Contributions

Electrical machinery and equipment	29%
Pharmaceuticals	24
Paper and like products	8
Banking	8
Food, beverage, and tobacco	7

Median Percent of Total Contributions

Pharmaceuticals	5%
Finance	5
Printing and publishing	4
Chemicals	4
Electrical machinery and equipment	4

Aggregate Dollar Value of Contributions ($ Millions)

Electrical machinery and equipment	$109
Pharmaceuticals	$ 24
Food, beverage, and tobacco	$ 12
Chemicals	$ 9
Banking	$ 6

Median Dollar Value of Contributions ($ Thousands)

Pharmaceuticals	$486
Paper and like products	$193
Electrical machinery and equipment	$154
Food, beverage, and tobacco	$105
Telecommunications	$ 82

Chart 23:
Distribution of Corporate Contributions by Industry Sector

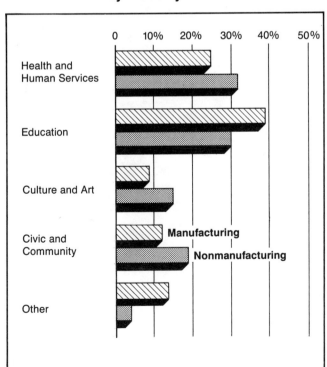

ably larger than they have been—24% of total contributions, compared to 9% in 1986 and 13% in 1984. Several of the pharmaceutical companies are among the top 75 donors, and many of them listed between 20% and 80% of their total contributions under the "other" category.

Additional industries with relatively high proportions of giving to "other" beneficiaries were paper (8%); banking (8%); food, beverage and tobacco (7%); and chemicals (7%).

Regional Giving

Regional figures are based on the headquarters region of the reporting company, not the location of the company facility actually making the donation or the destination of the funds donated. The data presented in Table 12 are consolidated figures for the company as a whole.

Certain identifiable differences have emerged over the four years that The Conference Board has collected and presented regional data. The major characteristics are as follows:

• Companies headquartered in the Mid-Atlantic region (New York and New Jersey) have consistently led all other regions in both median and aggregate total contributions. In 1987, their median contributions were $3.4 million, compared to $1.6 million nationally. Aggregate contributions in both the Mid-Atlantic and the Industrial Heartland were $479 million.

• Breadbasket-based corporations regained their position as the region with the highest contributions to domestic-pretax-income ratio. The ratio of 2.1% was double the average ratio for all survey respondents.

• Two regions reported high proportions of giving to education. Companies headquartered in the Pacific region gave an aggregate 45% of total contributions, and Mid-Atlantic companies gave 43 percent. Mid-Atlantic companies also gave the highest median dollar value to education, $943,000. Missing from the leaders in education were companies based in New England. Historically, this region has donated nearly half of its total contributions to education. However, because the $90-million dollar property gift to the "other" category came from a New England-based company, the figures for New England in 1987 are skewed.

• Breadbasket companies once again reported the highest proportion of giving to the arts (18%). The tradition of cultural giving in Minneapolis provides consistent leadership.

• In 1987, the Southwest states edged out the normally high civic and community giving by industrialized states in the Heartland; Pennsylvania, Ohio, Michigan, Indiana, Illinois, and Wisconsin. Contributions from companies headquartered in the Southwest were (23%), the Mountain states (19%), the Breadbasket (17%), and the Industrial Heartland (16%).

• The three western regions led in the percentage of giving to federated campaigns: Mountain (23%), Pacific (18%), and the Southwest (16%).

Table 10: Beneficiaries of Support Among 75 Largest Donors, 1987

Company Rank	Total Contributions (Dollars)	Health and Human Services	Education	Culture and Art	Civic and Community	Other
1	$136,415,202	7%	12%	4%	2%	75%
2	98,327,500	19	58	9	9	5
3	57,286,000	17	70	1	8	3
4	49,749,899	19	62	12	7	*
5	39,647,698	12	53	16	17	2
6	38,173,878	25	34	6	10	24
7	36,533,000	34	27	2	37	0
8	31,285,777	14	16	3	67	*
9	26,568,260	27	40	21	11	1
10	26,346,395	19	76	2	1	2
11	24,256,155	85	4	8	4	*
12	24,249,478	24	52	7	7	9
13	22,608,681	10	34	25	28	2
14	22,194,791	21	28	11	39	0
15	21,820,300	39	27	6	25	3
16	21,464,000	32	26	10	5	26
17	21,410,863	12	48	7	31	3
18	20,156,147	28	38	14	16	3
19	19,380,510	28	7	42	23	*
20	18,741,141	21	62	7	9	2
21	18,464,543	15	43	15	15	12
22	17,146,687	18	59	4	18	0
23	16,561,377	36	30	20	13	*
24	16,552,000	32	43	10	14	1
25	15,100,000	32	32	17	17	2
26	14,856,544	24	49	8	15	5
27	14,791,560	27	53	13	6	1
28	14.000,000	24	44	9	19	4
29	13,542,912	34	30	5	23	8
30	13,141,795	50	25	8	17	0
31	12,375,252	46	7	15	32	1
32	12,148,000	34	41	15	8	2
33	12,048,677	8	9	1	1	80
34	11,811,000	39	33	18	9	1
35	11,795,249	13	55	2	17	13
36	11,269,558	18	24	12	14	33
37	10,884,188	29	41	16	7	7
38	10,666,140	28	27	22	18	5
39	10,643,447	22	41	27	8	2
40	10,433,638	34	37	10	4	15
41	10,368,225	24	50	13	11	2
42	10,362,512	34	20	11	7	29
43	10,319,559	25	45	13	17	0
44	10,120,000	18	53	2	7	20
45	10,119,589	26	49	14	10	1
46	9,961,737	16	5	1	75	2
47	9,660,201	92	4	1	2	1
48	9,504,819	35	34	6	25	*
49	9,410,503	46	28	13	8	5
50	9,288,959	40	19	27	14	0

Total in a row may not add to 100 percent due to rounding.

*Less than 1 percent.
n.a. = Not available.

Table 10: Beneficiaries of Support Among 75 Largest Donors, 1987

Company Rank	Total Contributions (Dollars)	Health and Human Services	Education	Culture and Arts	Civic and Community	Other
51	9,213,670	39	29	11	21	*
52	9,062,725	28	33	20	19	0
53	9,033,495	43	32	8	16	2
54	8,900,000	51	19	24	7	0
55	8,415,214	26	26	37	11	0
56	8,411,591	9	89	1	*	0
57	8,369,443	42	33	22	1	3
58	8,267,635	26	40	12	17	4
59	8,099,883	36	38	10	17	0
60	8,063,854	25	38	17	19	1
61	7,828,684	31	31	14	14	9
62	7,700,000	28	28	15	30	0
63	7,496,118	35	47	7	10	1
64	7,404,991	79	15	4	2	0
65	7,305,421	28	33	14	14	11
66	7,060,000	13	60	9	18	0
67	6,906,164	33	39	10	7	12
68	6,747,240	16	41	19	24	0
69	6,690,176	12	46	2	11	29
70	6,659,064	n.a.	n.a.	n.a.	n.a.	n.a.
71	6,539,939	30	34	14	21	1
72	6,532,000	38	25	13	24	*
73	6,529,986	28	48	15	7	1
74	6,116,672	22	27	24	27	0
75	5,944,839	12	32	2	21	33

Total in a row may not add to 100 percent due to rounding.

* Less than 1 percent.

n.a. = Not available.

Table 11: Median Contribution to Federated Campaigns

Program Size	Number of Companies	Median Contribution to Federated Campaign
Less than $500,000	67	$ 70,710
$500,000 to $1 million	56	161,450
$1 million to $5 million	99	375,097
$5 million and over	71	1,554,500
Total	293	$ 292,770

Table 12: Distribution of Corporate Contributions by Headquarters Region, 1987

Region	Number of Companies	Total Contributions ($ millions)	Federated Campaigns	Other Health and Human Services	Total Health and Human Services	Education	Culture and Arts	Civic and Community	Other
				Health and Human Services					
New England .... (Maine, New Hampshire, Vermont, Massachusetts, Rhode Island, Connecticut)	31	$ 233.3	8%	7%	15%	22%	8%	10%	45%
Mid-Atlantic: .... (New York, New Jersey)	56	479.2	11	13	24	43	13	14	6
Industrial Heartland:................ (Pennsylvania, Ohio, Michigan, Indiana, Illinois, Wisconsin)	104	479.1	14	19	33	37	8	16	6
Southeast:....................... (Delaware, Maryland, Virginia, West Virginia, Kentucky, Tennessee, North Carolina, South Carolina, Georgia, Florida, Alabama, Mississippi)	44	135.4	11	18	29	38	12	11	10
Breadbasket:..................... (Minnesota, Iowa, Missouri, Kansas, Nebraska, South Dakota, North Dakota)	26	106.6	11	23	34	26	18	17	4
Southwest: .... (Arkansas, Louisiana, Texas, Oklahoma)	27	69.7	16	11	27	38	10	23	2
Mountain States: .... (Montana, Wyoming, Colorado, New Mexico, Arizona, Utah, Nevada, Idaho)	3	1.7	23	25	47	18	14	19	1
Pacific .... (Washington, Oregon, California, Alaska, Hawaii)	34	153.5	18	12	30	45	11	13	1
Total........................	325	$1,658.4	12%	15%	27%	37%	11%	14%	11%

[a]Total for a region may not add to 100 percent because of rounding.

Table 1: Corporate Contributions and Corporate Income Before and After Taxes[1]

Year	Amount ($ Millions)	Income[3] before Taxes ($ Millions)	As Percent of Income before Taxes	Income[3] after Taxes ($ Millions)	As Percent of Income after Taxes
1936	$ 30	$ 7,900	0.38%	$ 4,900	0.61%
1937	33	7,900	0.42	5,300	0.62
1938	27	4,100	0.65	2,900	0.93
1939	31	7,200	0.43	5,700	0.54
1940	38	10,000	0.38	7,200	0.53
1941	58	17,900	0.32	10,300	0.56
1942	98	21,700	0.45	10,300	0.95
1943	159	25,300	0.63	11,200	1.42
1944	234	24,200	0.97	11,300	2.07
1945	266	19,800	1.34	9,100	2.92
1946	214	24,800	0.86	15,700	1.36
1947	241	31,800	0.76	20,500	1.18
1948	239	35,600	0.67	23,200	1.03
1949	223	29,200	0.76	19,000	1.17
1950	252	42,900	0.59	25,000	1.01
1951	343	44,500	0.77	21,900	1.57
1952	399	39,600	1.01	20,200	1.98
1953	495	41,200	1.20	20,900	2.37
1954	314	38,700	0.81	21,100	1.49
1955	415	49,200	0.84	27,200	1.53
1956	418	49,600	0.84	27,600	1.51
1957	419	48,100	0.87	26,700	1.57
1958	395	41,900	0.94	22,900	1.72
1959	482	52,600	0.92	28,900	1.67
1960	482	49,800	0.97	27,100	1.78
1961	512	49,700	1.03	26,900	1.90
1962	595	55,000	1.08	31,100	1.91
1963	657	59,600	1.10	33,400	1.97
1964	729	66,500	1.10	38,500	1.89
1965	785	77,200	1.02	46,300	1.70
1966	805	83,000	0.97	49,400	1.63
1967	830	79,700	1.04	47,200	1.76
1968	1,005	88,500	1.13	49,400	2.03
1969	1,055	86,700	1.22	47,200	2.24
1970	797	75,400	1.06	41,300	1.93
1971	865	86,600	1.00	49,000	1.76
1972	1,009	100,600	1.00	58,900	1.71
1973	1,174	125,600	0.93	76,600	1.53
1974	1,200	136,700	0.88	85,100	1.41
1975	1,202	132,100	0.91	81,500	1.47
1976	1,487	166,300	0.89	102,500	1.45
1977	1,791	200,400	0.89	127,400	1.41
1978	2,084	233,500	0.89	150,000	1.39
1979	2,288	257,200	0.89	169,200	1.35
1980	2,359	237,100	0.99	152,300	1.55
1981	2,514	226,500	1.11	145,400	1.73
1982	2,906	169,600	1.71	106,500	2.73
1983	3,627	207,600	1.75	130,400	2.78
1984	4,057	240,000	1.69	146,100	2.78
1985	4,472	224,300	1.99	127,800	3.50
1986	4,600(est.)[2]	236,400	1.95	129,800	3.54
1987	$4,600(est.)[2]	$276,700	1.66	$142,900	3.22

[1]Reflects total consolidated corporate income before and after taxes.

[2]From Council for Aid to Education.

[3]The income figures on this table have been adjusted to coincide with recently updated data issued by the Department of Commerce. Thus, some of the figures in the income columns, and the ratios based upon them, will differ slightly from those published here previously.

Note: Figures in this table reflect contributions and income of all U.S. corporations. Figures in all other tables in this report are based solely on responses by survey participants.

Sources: Department of Commerce, Internal Revenue Service.

Table 2: Contributions as a Percent of Pretax Income, Quartiles, 1978 to 1987[1]

	Contributions as a Percent of U.S. Income			Contributions as a Percent of Worldwide Income		
	Lower Quartile	Median	Upper Quartile	Lower Quartile	Median	Upper Quartile
1978	0.36%	0.66%	1.20%	0.34%	0.58%	0.98%
1979	0.40	0.69	1.15	0.36	0.50	1.00
1980	0.40	0.73	1.34	0.37	0.66	1.16
1981	0.40	0.81	1.47	0.40	0.72	1.23
1982	0.54	1.13	1.85	0.53	0.99	1.62
1983	0.63	1.12	1.97	0.52	0.94	1.65
1984	0.56	1.03	1.88	0.53	0.85	1.54
1985	0.63	1.18	2.04	0.58	0.99	1.60
1986	0.66	1.17	2.18	0.59	1.01	1.63
1987	0.56	1.05	2.03	0.50	0.85	1.64

[1]In each table using medians or quartiles, the data for each group (e.g., an industry class, an asset or income-size group) are placed in rank order from the lowest to the highest value, and divided into quarters. The first quartile is 25 percent of the way from the bottom number in the ranking; the median is the middle value in the ranking; and the third quartile is then 75 percent of the way between the lowest and the highest value. The "total" line on each table provides the quartiles (or median) for all of the companies included in that table.

Table 3: Structure of Corporate Contributions, 1983-1987
(millions of dollars)

	1987	1986	1985	1984	1983
Total company contributions	$1,555.2 (315)	$1,688.6 (353)	$1,666.5 (423)	$1,448.9 (404)	$1,250.7 (484)
Less: Grants to company foundations	486.8 (129)	649.1 (157)	614.0 (182)	562.2 (157)	435.7 (159)
Other company contributions	1,068.5 (293)	1,039.5 (334)	1,052.5 (395)	886.7 (388)	815.0 (461)
Plus: Contributions by company foundations	609.9 (196)	641.0 (224)	658.4 (256)	569.2 (230)	553.0 (270)
Total corporate contributions	$1,678.3 (328)	$1,680.4 (372)	$1,710.9 (439)	$1,455.9 (422)	$1,368.0 (503)

(Numbers in parentheses are counts of non-zero answers).

Table 4: Relationship of Foundation Payouts to Pay-ins, 1983-1987
(millions of dollars)

Category	1987	1986	1985	1984	1983
Grants to company foundations	$486.8	$649.1	$614.0	$562.2	$435.7
Contributions by company foundations	609.9	641.0	658.4	569.2	553.0
Payouts less pay-ins	123.1	(8.1)	44.4	7.0	117.3
Percent payouts exceeded pay-ins	25.29%	−1.25%	7.23%	1.25%	26.92%

Table 5: Flow of Funds Into and Out of Company Foundations, 1983 to 1987

	1987		1986		1985		1984		1983	
	Number of Companies	Percent of Total	Number of Companies	Percent of Total	Number of Companies	Percent of Total	Number of Companies	Percent of Total	Number of Companies	Percent of Total
Pay-ins equal to payouts.......	26	12%	22	9%	25	9%	16	7%	7	2%
Pay-ins less than payouts	120	56	136	57	162	60	143	59	187	69
Pay-ins greater than payouts ...	67	32	82	34	82	30	84	34	78	29
Total	213	100%	240	100%	269	100%	243	100%	272	100%

Table 6: Contributions as a Percent of Pretax Income, 1987—
Companies Grouped by Rate of Giving

Contributions as Percent of Pretax Income	U.S. Pretax Income					
	All Companies	Manufacturing	Banking	Insurance[1]	Utilities and Telecommunication	Other Service
	(Number of Companies)[2]					
0- .24%	18	3	0	1	12	2
.25- .49	32	9	1	6	16	0
.50- .74	36	19	6	1	5	5
.75- .99	24	11	5	3	4	1
1.0-1.49	36	23	6	3	1	3
1.5-1.99	25	19	2	2	1	1
2.0-2.99	19	16	1	1	0	1
3.0-3.99	12	11	1	0	0	0
4.0-4.99	7	3	1	1	1	1
5.0 and over	19	13	0	5	1	0
Total	228	127	23	23	41	14

Contributions as Percent of Pretax Income	Worldwide Pretax Income					
	All Companies	Manufacturing	Banking	Insurance[1]	Utilities and Telecommunication	Other Service
	(Number of Companies)[3]					
0- .24%	20	4	0	1	12	3
.25- .49	45	18	1	6	18	2
.50- .74	51	33	4	2	6	6
.75- .99	34	23	4	3	3	1
1.0-1.49	38	25	4	4	1	4
1.5-1.99	26	19	0	2	4	1
2.0-2.99	19	11	4	3	0	1
3.0-3.99	9	6	3	0	0	0
4.0-4.99	9	4	0	1	2	2
5.0 and over	13	7	0	5	0	1
Total	264	150	20	27	46	21

[1] Insurance company figures are based on "net gain from operations after dividends to policyholders and before federal income tax, excluding capital gains and losses"—the closest measure to pretax income of corporations generally.

[2] 26 loss companies excluded.

[3] 24 loss companies excluded.

Table 7A: Contributions as a Percent of U.S. Pretax Income, 1987
Companies Grouped by Industry Class[1]

Industrial Classification	Number of Companies	U.S. Pretax Income (Sum) ($ Millions)	Contributions (Sum) ($ Thousands)	U.S. Pretax Income (Median) ($ Thousands)	Contributions (Median) ($ Thousands)	Contributions as a Percent of U.S. Pretax Income (Median)
Chemicals	21	$ 8,547	$ 129,875	$ 172,197	$2,470	1.40%
Electrical machinery and equipment	20	11,782	359,587	246,450	3,046	1.71
Food, beverage and tobacco	18	8,077	158,383	329,276	5,943	2.06
Machinery, nonelectrical	8	740	8,725	32,188	682	1.42
Paper and like products	9	2,628	23,275	229,600	1,164	0.53
Petroleum and gas[2]	11	10,338	140,143	781,000	10,320	1.31
Pharmaceuticals	8	4,546	87,397	435,850	9,532	1.67
Manufacturing[3]	12	1,038	21,888	53,539	651	2.66
Printing and publishing	6	1,923	19,709	281,638	3,746	0.86
Textiles and apparel	3	404	2,516	*	*	*
Transportation equipment[4]	11	8,745	64,588	201,800	3,525	1.16
Total: Manufacturing	127	$ 58,768	$1,016,086	229,400	2,605	1.41
Banking	23	6,057	63,692	87,450	1,013	0.99
Business services[5]	2	129	713	*	*	*
Finance	4	1,181	9,415	*	*	*
Insurance[6]	23	4,716	37,818	41,199	775	1.03
Retail and wholesale trade	5	2,507	43,706	255,000	1,725	0.96
Telecommunications	6	10,252	54,877	1,909,150	8,431	0.49
Transportation	3	222	2,560	*	*	*
Utilities	35	12,587	37,182	207,235	716	0.32
Total: Nonmanufacturing	101	$ 37,651	$ 249,963	129,045	853	0.71
Total: All Companies	228	$ 96,419	$1,266,049	187,404	1,499	1.05

[1]Loss companies excluded.

[2]Includes mining companies.

[3]Includes primary metal industries, fabricated metal products, and stone, clay and glass products.

[4]Includes tire manufactures.

[5]Includes engineering and construction companies.

[6]Insurance company figures are based on "net gain from operations after dividends to policyholders and before federal income tax, excluding capital gains and losses"— the closest measure to pretax income of corporations generally.

*Industries with fewer than 5 cases are excluded.

Table 7B: Contributions as a Percent of Worldwide Pretax Income, 1987
Companies Grouped by Industry Class[1]

Industrial Classification	Number of Companies	Worldwide Pretax Income (Sum) ($ Millions)	Contributions (Sum) ($ Thousands)	Worldwide Pretax Income (Median) ($ Thousands)	Contributions (Median) ($ Thousands)	Contributions as a Percent of Worldwide Pretax Income (Median)
Chemicals	22	$ 13,936	$ 130,710	$ 303,967	$1,970	0.79%
Electrical machinery and equipment	22	21,723	368,355	288,386	3,046	1.20
Food, beverage and tobacco	20	12,196	174,826	419,119	5,943	1.29
Machinery, nonelectrical	11	1,209	12,046	45,700	719	0.99
Paper and like products	11	4,240	31,023	336,100	2,610	0.67
Petroleum and gas[2]	18	26,266	186,260	267,500	7,084	0.94
Pharmaceuticals	9	7,791	90,124	937,125	9,411	1.03
Other Manufacturing[3]	12	1,741	21,888	97,444	651	1.18
Printing and publishing	8	2,809	30,094	308,585	3,696	0.82
Textiles and apparel	3	452	2,516	*	*	*
Transportation equipment[4]	14	15,725	124,306	159,820	1,914	0.88
Total: Manufacturing	150	$108,088	$1,172,148	290,914	2,610	0.95
Banking	20	2,123	30,944	78,041	855	1.07
Business services[5]	6	650	8,764	87,717	412	0.45
Finance	5	1,549	13,241	294,800	1,223	1.22
Insurance[6]	27	5,958	55,428	68,700	868	1.04
Retail and wholesale trade	6	3,653	44,757	343,997	1,128	0.81
Telecommunications	8	13,646	108,984	1,909,150	8,431	0.76
Transportation	4	543	4,315	*	*	*
Utilities	38	14,401	44,182	207,516	784	0.32
Total: Nonmanufacturing	114	$ 42,523	$ 310,615	138,217	868	0.72
Total: All Companies	264	$150,611	$1,482,763	236,655	1,591	0.85

[1]Loss companies excluded.

[2]Includes mining companies.

[3]Includes primary metal industries, fabricated metal products, and stone, clay and glass products.

[4]Includes tire manufacturers.

[5]Includes engineering and construction companies.

[6]Insurance company figures are based on "net gain from operations after dividends to policyholders and before federal income tax, excluding capital gains and losses"— the closest measure to pretax income of corporations generally.

*Industries with fewer than 5 cases are excluded.

Table 8A: Charitable Contributions of 75 Largest Donors as a Percent of U.S. and Worldwide Pretax Income, 1987

Company Rank	Contributions[1] (dollars)	U.S. Pretax Income[2] ($ Thousands)	Contributions as Percent of U.S. Pretax Income	Worldwide Pretax Income[2] ($ Thousands)	Contributions as Percent of Worldwide Pretax Income
1	$136,415,202	$ 2,700,000	5.07%	$ 3,200,000	4.25%
2	98,327,500	2,900,000	3.36	8,600,000	1.14
3	57,286,000	n.a.	n.a.	3,500,000	1.64
4	49,749,899	n.a.	n.a.	3,200,000	1.57
5	39,647,698	2,600,000	1.51	9,500,000	0.42
6	38,173,878	1,000,000	3.74	1,800,000	2.10
7	36,533,000	500,000	8.08	600,000	5.92
8	31,285,777	n.a.	n.a.	n.a.	n.a.
9	26,568,260	2,900,000	0.92	3,300,000	0.79
10	26,346,395	400,000	5.96	1,000,000	2.74
11	24,256,155	200,000	10.03	400,000	5.42
12	24,249,478	2,100,000	1.15	3,700,000	0.66
13	22,608,681	800,000	2.72	1,700,000	1.34
14	22,194,791	1,700,000	1.31	2,200,000	1.02
15	21,820,300	1,800,000	1.24	1,900,000	1.13
16	21,464,000	400,000	4.95	1,200,000	1.80
17	21,410,863	1,300,000	1.70	2,500,000	0.85
18	20,156,147	4,500,000	0.44	6,600,000	0.30
19	19,380,510	400,000	4.85	400,000	4.85
20	18,741,141	n.a.	n.a.	1,800,000	1.05
21	18,464,543	1,600,000	1.19	3,000,000	0.61
22	17,146,687	1,000,000	1.71	1,100,000	1.60
23	16,561,377	1,900,000	0.87	1,900,000	0.87
24	16,552,000	800,000	2.12	2,900,000	0.58
25	15,100,000	2,000,000	0.77	1,900,000	0.77
26	14,856,544	900,000	1.63	1,600,000	0.95
27	14,791,560	1,300,000	1.15	2,000,000	0.75
28	14,000,000	400,000	3.66	900,000	1.52
29	13,542,912	n.a.	n.a.	1,100,000	1.28
30	13,141,794	500,000	2.43	700,000	1.77
31	12,375,252	n.a.	n.a.	n.a.	n.a.
32	12,148,000	700,000	1.85	700,000	1.85
33	12,048,677	800,000	1.60	900,000	1.29
34	11,811,000	2,700,000	0.44	2,700,000	0.44
35	11,795,249	1,000,000	1.23	2,100,000	0.55
36	11,269,558	900,000	1.29	*	*
37	10,884,188	n.a.	n.a.	n.a.	n.a.
38	10,666,140	2,000,000	0.52	*	n.a.
39	10,643,447	600,000	1.69	1,100,000	0.99
40	10,433,638	600,000	1.89	800,000	1.37
41	10,368,225	200,000	5.53	500,000	2.07
42	10,362,512	400,000	2.79	600,000	1.74
43	10,319,559	1,600,000	0.64	1,700,000	0.62
44	10,120,000	800,000	1.22	1,400,000	0.72
45	10,119,589	1,900,000	0.54	2,200,000	0.46
46	9,961,737	300,000	2.90	500,000	1.87
47	9,660,201	400,000	2.73	600,000	1.70
48	9,504,819	1,000,000	0.95	1,000,000	0.93
49	9,410,503	900,000	1.08	1,100,000	0.84
50	9,288,959	n.a.	n.a.	400,000	2.58

[1]Direct giving and company foundation pay-outs included; grants made to and retained by company foundations are excluded.

[2]Domestic and worldwide pretax income rounded, percentages actual.

*Company showed loss.

n.a. = Not available.

Table 8A: Charitable Contributions of 75 Largest Donors as a Percent of U.S. and Worldwide Pretax Income, 1987 (continued)

Company Rank	Contributions[1] (dollars)	U.S. Pretax Income[2] ($ Thousands)	Contributions as Percent of U.S. Pretax Income	Worldwide Pretax Income[2] ($ Thousands)	Contributions as Percent of Worldwide Pretax Income
51	9,213,670	400,000	2.26	400,000	2.13
52	9,062,725	*	*	*	*
53	9,033,495	400,000	2.10	1,000,000	0.89
54	8,900,000	n.a.	n.a.	n.a.	n.a.
55	8,415,214	n.a.	n.a.	500,000	1.70
56	8,411,591	n.a.	n.a.	100,000	8.16
57	8,369,443	n.a.	n.a.	900,000	0.94
58	8,267,635	500,000	1.65	800,000	1.03
59	8,099,883	600,000	1.33	1,000,000	0.84
60	8,063,854	700,000	1.13	800,000	1.06
61	7,828,684	600,000	1.23	400,000	2.18
62	7,700,000	1,600,000	0.48	1,600,000	0.48
63	7,496,118	n.a.	n.a.	300,000	2.81
64	7,404,991	200,000	3.16	400,000	2.07
65	7,305,421	500,000	1.57	*	*
66	7,060,000	*	*	300,000	2.65
67	6,906,164	300,000	2.10	400,000	1.96
68	6,747,240	400,000	1.81	400,000	1.57
69	6,690,176	400,000	1.89	400,000	1.52
70	6,658,064	*	*	*	*
71	6,539,939	*	*	*	*
72	6,532,000	400,000	1.67	600,000	1.14
73	6,529,986	300,000	2.13	400,000	1.57
74	6,116,672	n.a.	n.a.	100,000	4.43
75	5,944,839	n.a.	n.a.	n.a.	n.a.

[1]Direct giving and company foundation pay-outs included; grants made to and retained by company foundations are excluded.

[2]Domestic and worldwide pretax income rounded, percentages actual.

*Company showed loss.

n.a. = Not available.

Table 8B: Corporate Social Expenditure of 75 Largest Donors as a Percent of U.S. and Worldwide Pretax Income, 1987

Company Rank	Total Corporate Social Expenditure	Corporate Social Expenditure As a Percent of		Rank for Corporate Assistance Only	Rank for Cash Only
		U.S. Pretax Income	Worldwide Pretax Income		
1	$142,874,145	5.31	4.46	7	2
2	122,127,500	4.17	1.42	1	1
3	57,286,000	n.a.	n.a.	137	4
4	49,749,899	n.a.	1.57	141	5
5	42,053,965	1.46	1.26	3	7
6	40,785,877	1.55	0.43	32	3
7	39,130,951	3.84	2.15	36	6
8	36,533,000	8.08	5.92	209	14
9	34,042,112	n.a.	n.a.	20	24
10	32,065,201	9.05	5.64	2	163
11	26,346,395	5.96	2.74	191	65
12	25,678,679	1.35	1.35	4	17
13	25,422,478	1.21	0.69	29	8
14	24,806,155	10.25	5.54	46	74
15	23,578,791	1.39	1.09	28	16
16	22,608,681	2.72	1.34	181	33
17	22,542,000	5.19	1.89	34	21
18	22,201,000	n.a.	2.10	5	23
19	21,820,300	1.24	1.13	161	9
20	21,410,863	1.70	0.85	193	10
21	20,449,000	2.62	0.71	13	18
22	20,156,147	0.44	0.30	201	12
23	19,380,510	4.85	4.85	145	11
24	18,741,141	n.a.	1.05	177	13
25	18,464,543	1.19	0.61	153	15
26	17,747,493	1.77	1.66	43	36
27	17,345,580	2.64	2.64	11	25
28	16,337,000	1.97	1.16	8	46
29	15,279,854	1.68	0.98	50	37
30	15,100,000	0.77	0.77	185	19
31	14,889,640	1.16	0.75	95	20
32	14,125,195	1.62	*	17	28
33	14,000,000	3.66	1.52	169	22
34	13,187,241	n.a.	n.a.	37	78
35	13,141,794	2.43	1.77	165	38
36	12,995,923	2.13	1.35	12	49
37	12,957,950	3.94	3.68	9	58
38	12,382,632	1.23	1.21	16	39
39	12,048,677	1.60	1.29	190	109
40	11,836,629	6.32	2.36	26	35
41	11,811,000	0.44	0.44	157	26
42	11,795,249	1.23	0.55	173	27
43	11,423,854	1.61	1.50	14	50
44	10,995,538	2.96	1.85	42	57
45	10,884,188	n.a.	n.a.	139	29
46	10,666,140	0.52	*	189	30
47	10,643,447	1.69	0.99	149	31
48	10,433,638	1.89	1.37	197	32
49	10,319,559	0.64	0.62	205	34
50	10,119,589	0.54	0.46	211	54

*Company showed loss.

n.a. = Not available.

Table 8B: Corporate Social Expenditure of 75 Largest Donors as a Percent of U.S. and Worldwide Pretax Income, 1987 (continued)

Company Rank	Total Corporate Social Expenditure	Corporate Social Expenditure As a Percent of		Rank for Corporate Assistance Only	Rank for Cash Only
		U.S. Pretax Income	Worldwide Pretax Income		
51	9,961,737	2.90	1.87	251	114
52	9,886,748	n.a.	1.11	25	48
53	9,410,503	1.08	0.84	171	40
54	9,367,653	n.a.	2.60	97	41
55	9,213,670	2.26	2.13	147	51
56	9,062,725	*	*	203	42
57	9,033,495	2.10	0.89	215	44
58	8,900,000	n.a.	n.a.	155	43
59	8,640,226	5.04	2.25	6	133
60	8,415,214	n.a.	1.70	187	45
61	8,411,591	n.a.	8.16	291	120
62	8,267,635	1.65	1.03	163	47
63	7,986,564	n.a.	0.60	15	72
64	7,828,684	1.23	2.18	195	52
65	7,740,386	3.30	2.16	54	97
66	7,700,000	0.48	0.48	179	53
67	7,496,118	n.a.	2.81	151	55
68	7,365,104	1.92	*	21	69
69	7,305,421	1.57	*	183	56
70	7,239,939	*	*	40	62
71	7,220,000	*	2.71	76	61
72	6,952,787	1.96	1.58	61	73
73	6,747,240	1.81	1.57	167	59
74	6,658,064	*	*	199	60
75	6,532,000	1.67	1.14.	159	63

*Company showed loss.

n.a. = Not available.

Table 9A: Contributions as a Percent of U.S. Pretax Income, 1987—
Companies Grouped by Dollar Size of Program

Program Size	Number of Companies	Lower Quartile	Median	Upper Quartile
Under $500,000	47	0.33%	0.61%	1.25%
$500,000 to $1 million	50	0.39	0.77	1.52
$1 million to $5 million	72	0.62	0.97	1.74
$5 million and over	59	1.15	1.67	2.73
All Groups	228	0.56	1.05	2.03

Table 9B: Contributions as a Percent of Worldwide Pretax Income, 1987—
Companies Grouped by Dollar Size of Program

Program Size	Number of Companies	Lower Quartile	Median	Upper Quartile
Under $500,000	52	0.33%	0.64%	1.24%
$500,000 to $1 million	53	0.37	0.71	1.57
$1 million to $5 million	92	0.55	0.80	1.41
$5 million and over	67	0.84	1.28	1.99
All Groups	264	0.50	0.85	1.64

Table 10A: Contributions as a Percent of U.S. Pretax Income—Quartile Rank, 1987
Companies Grouped by Size of U.S. Income

| U.S. Pretax Income | Number of Companies | Contributions Ratios[1] | | |
		Lower Quartile	Median	Upper Quartile[2]
Below $5 million	5	8.19	13.14	23.71
$5-9.9 million	7	3.34	6.39	14.66
$10-24.9 million	15	0.87	2.73	5.07
$25-49.9 million	22	0.70	1.24	2.19
$50-99.9 million	32	0.57	0.90	1.84
$100-249.9 million	50	0.48	0.75	1.24
$250-499.9 million	41	0.55	0.96	2.12
$500-999.9 million	31	0.30	1.13	1.63
$1 billion and over	25	0.46	0.92	1.41
All Income Groups	**228**	**0.56**	**1.05**	**2.03**

[1]The statistics presented here are derived only from companies with positive income.
[2]This is the 75th percentile.

Table 10B: Contributions as a Percent of Worldwide Pretax Income—Quartile Rank, 1987
Companies Grouped by Size of Worldwide Income

| Worldwide Pretax Income | Number of Companies | Contributions Ratios[1] | | |
		Lower Quartile	Median	Upper Quartile[2]
Below $5 million	5	8.92	22.02	41.65
$5-9.9 million	6	3.19	5.78	16.97
$10-24.9 million	16	0.91	1.98	3.12
$25-49.9 million	25	0.72	1.25	3.20
$50-99.9 million	33	0.55	0.98	1.69
$100-249.9 million	49	0.41	0.68	1.00
$250-499.9 million	56	0.44	0.81	1.51
$500-999.9 million	36	0.31	0.76	1.48
$1 billion and over	38	0.47	0.82	1.13
All Income Groups	**264**	**0.50**	**0.85**	**1.64**

[1]The statistics presented here are derived only from companies with positive income.
[2]This is the 75th percentile.

Table 11A: Contributions as a Percent of U.S. Pretax Income—Quartile Rank, 1987
Companies Grouped by Industry Class (with at least five cases in each)

| Industrial Classification | Number of Companies | Contributions Ratios[1] | | |
		Lower Quartile	Median	Upper Quartile[2]
Chemicals	21	1.07%	1.40%	1.93%
Electrical machinery and equipment	20	0.84	1.71	4.72
Food, beverage and tobacco	18	0.87	2.06	3.21
Machinery, nonelectrical	8	0.98	1.42	3.19
Paper and like products	9	0.37	0.53	1.02
Petroleum and gas[3]	11	0.67	1.31	1.70
Pharmaceuticals	8	1.32	1.67	2.62
Other manufacturing[4]	12	0.57	2.66	1.88
Printing and publishing	6	0.68	0.86	1.17
Transportation equipment[5]	11	0.68	1.16	1.85
Banking	23	0.72	0.99	1.46
Insurance	23	0.41	1.03	4.95
Retail and wholesale trade	5	0.70	0.96	3.04
Telecommunications	6	0.36	0.49	0.80
Utilities	35	0.18	0.32	0.62

[1]The statistics presented here are derived only from companies with positive income.
[2]This is the 75th percentile.
[3]Includes mining companies.
[4]Includes primary metal industries, fabricated metal products, and stone, clay and glass products.
[5]Includes tire manufacturers.

Table 11B: Contributions as a Percent of Worldwide Pretax Income—Quartile Rank, 1987
Companies Grouped by Industry Class (with at least five cases in each)

| Industrial Classification | Number of Companies | Contributions Ratios[1] | | |
		Lower Quartile	Median	Upper Quartile[2]
Chemicals	22	0.53%	0.79%	1.28%
Electrical machinery and equipment	22	0.70	1.20	1.85
Food, beverage and tobacco	20	0.80	1.29	2.04
Machinery, nonelectrical	11	0.70	0.99	1.47
Paper and like products	11	0.39	0.67	0.73
Petroleum and gas[3]	18	0.62	0.94	1.95
Pharmaceuticals	9	0.87	1.03	1.63
Other manufacturing[4]	12	0.33	1.18	3.45
Printing and publishing	8	0.62	0.82	1.71
Transportation equipment[5]	14	0.60	0.88	2.21
Banking	20	0.76	1.07	2.09
Business services[6]	6	0.32	0.45	17.80
Finance	5	0.37	1.22	1.44
Insurance	27	0.49	1.04	2.73
Retail and wholesale trade	6	0.41	0.81	2.06
Telecommunications	8	0.45	0.76	1.39
Utilities	38	0.21	0.32	0.63

[1]The statistics presented here are derived only from companies with positive income.
[2]This is the 75th percentile.
[3]Includes mining companies.
[4]Includes primary metal industries, fabricated metal products, and stone, clay and glass products.
[5]Includes tire manufacturers.
[6]Includes engineering and construction companies.

Table 12A: Contributions as a Percent of U.S. Pretax Income—Quartile Rank, 1987
Companies Grouped by Size of U.S. Assets

Assets	Number of Companies	Contributions' Ratios[1]		
		Lower Quartile	Median	Upper Quartile[2]
Below $100 million	0	*	*	*
$100-199 million	6	1.69%	4.18%	10.54%
$200-299 million	5	0.55	0.71	6.54
$300-499 million	9	0.93	1.05	2.31
$500-999 million	25	0.62	1.12	2.48
$1-1.9 billion	42	0.40	1.10	1.76
$2-2.9 billion	17	0.64	1.22	2.43
$3-3.9 billion	12	0.28	0.80	1.83
$4-4.9 billion	12	1.00	2.17	6.28
$5-9.9 billion	33	0.32	0.83	1.68
$10 billion and over	44	0.44	0.93	1.68
All Asset Groups	**205**	**0.53**	**1.06**	**2.10**

[1]The statistics presented here are derived only from companies with positive income.
[2]This is the 75th percentile.

Table 12B: Contributions as a Percent of Worldwide Pretax Income—Quartile Rank, 1987
Companies Grouped by Size of Worldwide Assets

Assets	Number of Companies	Contributions' Ratios[1]		
		Lower Quartile	Median	Upper Quartile[2]
Below $100 million	0	*	*	*
$100-199 million	3	*	*	*
$200-299 million	6	0.52%	1.07%	2.49%
$300-499 million	12	0.53	1.01	1.81
$500-999 million	26	0.62	1.10	2.43
$1-1.9 billion	40	0.40	0.72	1.23
$2-2.9 billion	25	0.44	0.79	2.12
$3-3.9 billion	18	0.30	0.95	1.91
$4-4.9 billion	18	0.68	0.86	2.53
$5-9.9 billion	50	0.43	0.82	1.50
$10 billion and over	63	0.46	0.87	1.57
All Asset Groups	**261**	**0.50**	**0.85**	**1.62**

[1]The statistics presented here are derived only from companies with positive income.
[2]This is the 75th percentile.
*Categories with fewer than 5 cases are excluded.

Table 13A: Contributions as a Percent of U.S. Pretax Income, 1987
Companies Grouped by Size of U.S. Sales

U.S. Sales	Number of Companies	Lower Quartile	Median	Upper Quartile
Below $250 million	8	0.80	2.16	5.50
$250-$500 million	16	0.50	0.87	1.70
$500 million-$1 billion	37	0.50	0.94	1.60
$1 billion-$2.5 billion	55	0.30	0.78	1.70
$2.5 billion-$5 billion	37	0.40	0.96	1.90
$5 billion and over	49	0.80	1.51	2.60

Table 13B: Contributions as a Percent of Worldwide Pretax Income, 1987
Companies Grouped by Size of Worldwide Sales

Worldwide Sales	Number of Companies	Lower Quartile[2]	Median	Upper Quartile
Below $250 million	6	0.70	1.08	9.00
$250-$500 million	16	0.60	1.04	1.80
$500 million-$1 billion	45	0.50	0.94	1.60
$1 billion-$2.5 billion	67	0.40	0.71	1.50
$2.5 billion-$5 billion	53	0.50	0.82	1.60
$5 billion and over	76	0.60	0.93	1.60
Total	263			

Table 14: Comparison of Corporate Contributions, 1987 and 1986
256 Companies Reporting in Both Years

Beneficiary	1987		1986		Median Percent Change 1986-1987
	Median Contributions Expenditure	Contributions to Beneficiary as Percent of Total Contributions (Median)	Median Contributions Expenditure	Contributions to Beneficiary as Percent of Total Contributions (Median)	
Health and human services	$ 598,691	36.9%	$ 562,000	37.2%	0.7%
Education	469,989	30.5	521,746	32.2	2.0
Culture and art	134,343	10.2	153,358	10.6	0.6
Civic and community	166,185	10.8	154,260	11.0	1.5
Other	41,351	2.3	38,750	2.1	0.8
Total	$1,591,000	a	$1,464,756	a	1.8%

[a]Since subcategory percentages are medians rather than sums, they do not add to 100 percent.

Table 15: Beneficiaries of Company Support, 1987—
Quartiles for Companies Grouped by Dollar Size of Program

Program Size	Number of Companies	Health and Human Services			Education			Culture and Art		
		Lower Quartile	Median	Upper Quartile	Lower Quartile	Median	Upper Quartile	Lower Quartile	Median	Upper Quartile
Less than $500,000	74	33.8%	47.5%	57.9%	15.6%	21.3%	32.4%	5.8%	10.9%	19.8%
$500,000 to $1 million	62	31.2	41.7	57.3	17.3	26.8	37.9	5.0	9.4	14.2
$1 million to $5 million	110	24.3	35.0	44.9	21.3	32.1	41.6	6.1	10.2	16.7
$5 million and over	79	18.3	27.6	35.8	26.9	33.4	46.8	6.2	11.0	15.4
All Groups	325	25.9	36.6	48.2	18.8	29.4	40.8	6.0	10.3	16.5

Table 15: Beneficiaries of Company Support, 1987 (continued)

Program Size	Number of Companies	Civic and Community			Other		
		Lower Quartile	Median	Upper Quartile	Lower Quartile	Median	Upper Quartile
Less than $500,000	74	5.6%	10.6%	15.2%	0.4%	2.4%	9.1%
$500,000 to $1 million	62	6.9	12.7	18.4	1.1	2.3	5.9
$1 million to $5 million	110	6.4	11.0	16.3	1.0	2.5	7.9
$5 million and over	79	7.4	13.8	19.0	0.9	2.3	9.0
All Companies	325	6.7	11.2	17.4	0.9	2.4	7.7

Table 16: Beneficiaries of Corporate Support, 1978 to 1987

	1987 325 Companies		1986 370 Companies		1985 436 Companies		1984 415 Companies	
	Thousands of Dollars	% of Total	Thousands of Dollars	% of Total	Thousands of Dollars	% of Total	Thousands of Dollars	% of Total
Health and Human Services								
Federated giving	$ 203,582	12.3%	$ 225,944	13.5			$ 193,891	13.4%
Hospitals	31,071	1.9	27,620	1.6			31,758	2.2
Matching gifts for health and human services	4,439	0.3	5,527	0.3			3,565	0.2
All other health and human services	146,441	8.8	167,320	10.0			128,626	8.9
Subcategories unspecified	64,982	3.9	42,239	2.5			42,107	2.9
Total health and human services	$ 450,515	27.2%	$ 468.650	28.0%	$ 494,109	29.2%	$ 399,948	27%
Education								
Higher education	290,873	17.5	400,405	23.9			283,375	19.6
Precollege education	25,232	1.5	30,873	1.8			22,366	1.5
Scholarships and fellowships	39,934	2.4	37,145	2.2			22,991	1.6
Education-related organizations	33,779	2.0	30,688	1.8			28,774	2.0
Matching gifts for education	108,257	6.5	107,436	6.4			75,994	5.3
Other	64,951	3.9	44,932	2.7			70,221	4.0
Subcategories unspecified	47,121	2.8	66,504	4.0			57,949	4.0
Total education	$ 610,146	36.8%	$ 717,983	42.9%	$ 650,005	38.3%	$ 561,670	38.9%
Culture and Art								
Matching gifts for culture and art	13,601	0.8	14,782	0.9			8,928	0.6
All other culture and art	151,533	9.1	144,953	8.7			123,233	8.5
Subcategories unspecified	13,471	0.8	39,019	2.3			22,549	1.6
Total culture and art	$ 178,605	10.8%	$ 198,754	11.9%	$ 187,536	11.1%	$ 154,711	10.7%
Civic and Community								
Public policy organizations	22,004	1.3	15,711	0.9			15,334	1.1
Community improvement	53,356	3.2	72,622	4.3			62,034	4.3
Environment and ecology	44,026	2.7	35,953	2.1			97,113	6.7
Justice and law	6,808	0.4	7,033	0.4			$ 6,109	0.4
Housing	6,395	0.4	8,237	0.5			14,378	1.0
Other	61,956	3.7	35,155	2.1			44,028	3.0
Subcategories unspecified	41,580	2.5	45,678	2.7			32,606	2.3
Total civic and community	$ 236,124	14.2%	$ 220,479	13.2%	$ 279,508	16.5%	$ 271,602	18.8%
Other								
Total other	$ 182,992	11.0%	$ 68,119	4.1%	$ 83,549	4.9%	$ 56,383	3.9%
Grand total	$1,658,382	100.0%	$1,673,985	100.0%	$1,694,707	100.0%	$1,444,313	100.0%

When data for 1987 were collected, many of the subcategories of the five beneficiaries of corporate support were combined to reduce the complexity of reporting and to provide a clear summary of the major subcategories.

The data from previous years in Table 16 has been restated to correspond to the combined subcategories introduced in 1987.

Subcategories may not add to totals due to rounding.

Table 16: Beneficiaries of Corporate Support, 1978 to 1987 (continued)

	1983 471 Companies		1982 534 Companies		1981 788 Companies		1980[1] 732 Companies		1979 786 Companies		1978 750 Companies	
	Thousands of Dollars	% of Total	Thousands of Dollars	% of Total	Thousands of Dollars	% of Total	Thousands of Dollars	% of Total	Thousands of Dollars	% of Total	Thousands of Dollars	% of Total
			$ 182,384	14.2%			$170,652	17.2%			$142,085	20.5%
			37,679	2.9			40,911	4.1			30,686	4.4
			2,157	0.2			749	0.1			292	0.0
			175,087	13.7			91,697	9.2			62,956	9.1
				0.0			33,857	3.4			19,832	2.0
	$ 267,300	28.7%	$ 397,307	31.0%	$ 393,309	33.6%	$337,866	34.0%	$292,641	35.0%	$255,851	36.9%
			259,294	20.2			197,143	19.8			143,485	20.7
			14,028	1.1			9,287	0.9			5,209	0.8
			34,568	2.7			31,180	3.1			20,353	2.9
			52,054	4.1			33,305	3.3			23,075	3.3
			76,364	6.0			48,821	4.9			27,081	3.9
			40,908	3.2			21,464	2.2			17,649	2.5
			44,997	3.5			34,647	3.5			19,408	2.8
	$ 498,800	39.0%	$ 522,213	40.7%	$ 429,810	36.7%	$375,847	37.8%	$314,845	37.7%	$256,260	37.0%
			4,312	0.3			2,065	0.2			402	0.1
			120,972	9.4			95,608	9.6			63,665	9.2
			120,972	9.4			95,608	9.6			63,665	9.0
			20,554	1.6			11,000	1.1			5,939	0.9
	$ 145,200	11.4%	$ 145,838	11.4%	$ 139,620	11.9%	$108,673	10.9%	$ 82,509	9.9	$ 70,006	10.1%
			15,220	1.2			16,031	1.6			7,921	1.1
			48,214	3.8			47,034	4.7			28,779	4.2
			13,783	1.1			10,794	1.1			11,190	1.6
			7,001	0.5			6,065	0.6			3,317	0.5
			12,751	1.0			7,711	0.8			5,627	0.8
			27,683	2.2			14,863	1.5			11,714	1.7
			24,600	1.9			14,290	1.4			10,464	1.5
	$ 188,800	14.8%	$ 149,252	11.6%	$136,647	11.7%	$116,788	11.7%	$ 97,345	11.6%	$ 79,012	11.4%
	$ 78,000	6.1%	$ 66,998	5.2%	$ 71,304	6.1%	$ 55,451	5.6%	$ 48,256	5.8%	$ 32,043	4.6%
	$1,278,100	100.0%	$1,281,608	100.0%	$170,690	100.0%	$994,625	100.0%	$835,596	100.0%	$693,172	100.0%

Table 17: Beneficiaries of Company Support, 1987—Quartiles for Companies Grouped by Industry Class[1]

Industry Category	Number of Companies	Health and Human Services			Education		
		Lower Quartile	Median	Upper Quartile	Lower Quartile	Median	Upper Quartile
Chemicals	25	24.6%	29.3%	37.5%	34.2%	40.3%	51.5%
Electrical machinery and equipment	23	9.2	23.6	28.9	37.9	48.1	74.2
Food, beverage and tobacco	20	30.2	41.1	66.6	19.5	29.0	37.0
Machinery, nonelectrical	13	31.8	43.1	51.9	18.1	29.5	45.4
Paper	13	17.6	31.6	42.8	25.1	33.5	48.5
Petroleum and gas[2]	22	20.6	27.9	36.6	33.2	44.1	54.1
Pharmaceuticals	11	15.2	32.1	42.2	19.9	32.1	45.6
Other manufacturing[3]	16	28.6	38.3	54.5	17.2	35.6	47.4
Printing and publishing	13	23.4	33.9	42.9	16.5	26.3	42.4
Textiles and apparel	5	33.2	40.9	50.6	20.9	36.5	38.5
Transportation equipment[4]	16	23.3	34.0	46.1	26.5	38.1	46.0
Total: Manufacturing	177	23.6	32.8	42.7	26.3	37.2	48.1
Banking	37	31.5	46.2	55.4	17.3	22.9	27.6
Business services[5]	8	18.1	36.1	54.2	10.7	28.0	47.3
Finance	8	17.8	22.2	36.6	14.8	20.9	39.2
Insurance	32	26.4	41.7	50.0	17.7	21.6	33.7
Retail and wholesale trade	8	29.7	41.2	50.1	13.7	18.9	37.8
Telecommunications	8	16.8	26.1	35.2	20.2	31.0	37.0
Transportation	5	31.9	53.7	69.8	14.5	17.8	34.5
Utilities	42	38.1	52.0	63.0	16.1	20.4	28.5
Total: Nonmanufacturing	148	29.4	43.2	57.0	16.9	22.2	30.2
Total: All Companies	325	25.9	36.6	48.2	18.8	29.4	40.8

[1]For an explanation of quartiles, see Table 2.
[2]Includes mining companies.
[3]Includes primary metal industries, fabricated metal products, and stone, clay and glass products.
[4]Includes tire manufacturers.
[6]Includes engineering and construction companies.

Table 17: Beneficiaries of Company Support, 1987 (continued)

Culture and Art			Civic and Community			Other		
Lower Quartile	Median	Upper Quartile	Lower Quartile	Median	Upper Quartile	Lower Quartile	Median	Upper Quartile
4.0%	8.7%	13.5%	7.4%	13.2%	17.1%	1.0%	3.9%	9.9%
3.1	5.3	14.6	1.9	6.4	9.7	1.4	3.8	11.4
4.3	7.7	10.5	6.7	11.6	16.5	1.0	1.5	9.6
6.3	10.6	15.6	4.8	10.6	14.5	0.3	1.0	6.1
4.7	8.3	12.8	7.8	10.4	35.6	1.2	2.6	11.6
6.5	10.3	14.4	11.1	14.9	18.8	0.6	0.9	2.7
2.1	7.3	10.8	5.0	7.8	15.5	2.7	5.2	29.0
4.4	9.2	19.4	3.9	6.6	7.6	1.4	2.6	6.9
13.3	19.0	23.4	7.9	11.2	15.9	0.8	4.0	10.9
2.2	9.5	21.7	9.1	13.2	17.6	2.7	3.7	8.3
6.1	11.0	16.2	8.0	10.4	15.5	1.5	2.2	3.6
5.1	9.5	14.4	6.4	10.3	15.6	1.1	2.6	7.9
9.8	12.8	19.1	9.9	13.8	19.5	1.4	2.3	7.6
2.8	10.4	20.4	4.2	14.8	31.1	0.7	1.7	7.5
14.5	17.2	23.6	11.6	20.3	33.8	1.0	4.6	19.0
6.1	14.7	19.5	6.3	12.1	20.1	0.3	2.3	8.4
6.3	8.5	25.2	6.0	13.8	24.3	0.7	2.3	5.9
15.2	19.4	31.1	8.2	14.5	18.7	0.5	2.0	6.5
2.7	19.0	30.8	4.6	8.1	15.2	1.6	2.1	2.5
4.9	8.0	12.5	6.9	12.0	18.6	0.3	2.6	7.3
7.3	11.5	19.2	6.9	13.2	20.5	0.6	2.3	7.2
6.0	10.3	16.5	6.7	11.2	17.4	0.9	2.4	7.7

Table 18: Beneficiaries of Company Support, 1987—Companies Grouped by Industry Class (with at least five cases in each)

			Health and Human Services					
Industrial Classification	Number of Companies	Total Contributions ($ Thousands)	Federated Giving	Hospitals	Matching Gifts	All Other Health and Human Services	Unspecified	Total Health and Human Service
Chemicals	25	$ 137,615	10.1	2.7	0.2	13.7	1.1	27.7
Electrical machinery and equipment ...	23	373,177	10.4	1.3	0.3	2.5	0.1	14.8
Food, beverage and tobacco	20	174,826	5.4	1.1	0.5	19.4	19.4	45.7
Machinery, nonelectrical	13	14,822	27.8	1.7	1.1	6.9	2.1	39.6
Paper and like products	13	32,747	15.5	2.0	*	7.0	—	24.5
Petroleum and gas[a]	22	203,220	11.8	1.8	0.2	6.4	1.5	21.8
Pharmaceuticals	11	96,678	9.2	2.5	0.2	13.5	2.2	27.5
Other manufacturing[b]	16	23,439	11.3	2.5	—	11.7	3.0	28.5
Printing and publishing	13	44,066	9.9	0.9	*	12.3	10.2	33.2
Textiles and apparel	5	3,407	28.4	1.2	—	13.0	—	42.5
Transportation equipment[c]	16	126,807	14.1	3.2	—	6.9	0.3	24.6
Total: Manufacturing	177	1,230,805	10.6	1.8	0.3	8.8	3.8	25.3
Banking	37	81,893	17.2	3.2	0.4	10.9	4.5	36.2
Business services[d]	8	14,095	11.8	1.0	—	11.8	—	24.5
Finance	8	19,774	9.0	0.6	0.2	8.7	2.6	21.2
Insurance	32	93,613	15.6	2.4	0.4	10.9	0.8	30.1
Retail and wholesale trade	8	54,144	22.8	1.0	0.2	8.4	4.0	36.4
Telecommunications	8	108,984	13.1	1.2	*	3.1	8.6	25.9
Transportation	5	4,466	31.1	0.9	0.2	7.4	1.5	41.1
Utilities	42	50,608	26.4	2.7	0.8	13.5	2.7	46.1
Total: Nonmanufacturing	148	427,577	17.2	2.0	0.3	8.8	4.2	32.4
Total: All Companies	325	$1,658,382	12.3	1.9	0.3	8.8	3.9	27.2

[a] Includes mining companies.
[b] Includes primary metal industries, fabricated metal products, and stone, clay and glass products.
[c] Includes tire manufacturers.
[d] Includes engineering and construction companies.
*Less than 1 percent.
Details in a row may not add to total due to rounding.

Table 18: Beneficiaries of Company Support, 1987—Companies Grouped by Industry Class (with at least five cases in each) (continued)

			Education					
Industrial Classification	Higher Education	Precollege Education	Scholarships and Fellowships	Education-Related Organization	Matching Gifts	Other	Unspecified Unspecified	Education[1] Education[1]
Chemicals	20.7	1.4	3.3	2.2	6.2	2.7	5.0	41.5
Electrical machinery and equipment	26.1	2.2	2.4	1.4	5.8	2.7	0.6	41.3
Food, beverage and tobacco	7.2	0.4	2.9	2.0	4.8	6.6	3.1	27.0
Machinery, nonelectrical	14.0	0.6	5.6	2.9	9.1	2.4	—	34.6
Paper and like products	12.5	3.3	3.2	1.9	3.8	0.6	—	25.3
Petroleum and gas	17.5	2.2	3.5	3.1	12.2	2.3	4.3	45.0
Pharmaceuticals	17.4	0.8	3.3	2.7	5.5	0.6	2.7	32.9
Other manufacturing	16.4	1.0	3.3	3.3	9.0	0.4	2.9	36.4
Printing and publishing	12.3	0.7	1.7	3.1	6.9	0.7	0.6	26.0
Textiles and apparel	13.5	2.3	8.1	3.0	6.3	0.2	—	33.2
Transportation equipment	20.2	1.4	2.4	1.9	4.4	22.6	0.6	53.5
Total: Manufacturing	18.9	1.6	2.9	2.1	6.7	4.9	2.2	39.3
Banking	10.2	1.8	0.7	2.5	8.4	1.8	0.3	25.8
Business services	27.1	1.9	0.7	1.9	11.7	0.1	—	43.4
Finance	2.3	1.1	2.5	0.7	12.5	3.5	6.7	29.5
Insurance	9.0	2.0	1.2	1.5	6.8	1.4	1.1	23.0
Retail and wholesale trade	3.7	2.2	0.1	0.2	1.0	1.5	11.0	19.7
Telecommunications	25.7	0.2	1.1	2.5	5.9	0.2	9.0	44.5
Transportation	15.5	0.2	1.2	0.2	2.5	3.1	2.0	24.6
Utilities	13.0	0.9	1.3	1.4	3.1	0.2	2.1	22.0
Total: Nonmanufacturing	13.7	1.3	1.0	1.7	6.1	1.1	4.6	29.5
Total: All Companies	17.5	1.5	2.4	2.0	6.5	3.9	2.8	36.8

[1]See footnotes on page 50.

Table 18: Beneficiaries of Company Support, 1987—Companies Grouped by Industry Class (with at least five cases in each) (continued)

Industrial Classification	Matching Gifts	Culture and Art		Total Culture and Art[1]
		All Other Culture and Art	Unspecified	
Chemicals	0.5	5.4	0.2	6.1
Electrical machinery and equipment	1.1	6.2	*	7.3
Food, beverage and tobacco	0.6	7.8	0.6	9.0
Machinery, nonelectrical	1.3	8.3	0.1	9.7
Paper and like products	0.3	7.2	—	7.5
Petroleum and gas[a]	0.9	9.8	1.3	12.1
Pharmaceuticals	0.5	5.8	1.1	7.4
Other manufacturing[b]	0.7	22.4	0.5	23.6
Printing and publishing	1.8	18.9	—	20.7
Textiles and apparel	—	8.6	—	8.6
Transportation equipment[c]	0.5	8.5	0.2	9.2
Total: Manufacturing	0.8	8.0	0.4	9.2
Banking	1.2	14.0	1.1	16.2
Business services[d]	*	14.7	—	14.7
Finance	0.1	10.6	6.6	17.3
Insurance	0.6	9.0	1.3	10.9
Retail and wholesale trade	0.3	19.4	2.5	22.2
Telecommunications	1.0	12.8	2.7	16.4
Transportation	7.6	16.3	0.1	23.9
Utilities	0.8	8.5	0.6	9.9
Total: Nonmanufacturing	0.8	12.5	1.9	15.2
Total: All Companies	0.8	9.1	0.8	10.8

[1]See footnotes on page 54.

Table 18: Beneficiaries of Company Support, 1987—Companies Grouped by Industry Class (with at least five cases in each) (continued)

Industrial Classification	Public Policy Organizations	Community Improvement	Civic and Community					Total Civic and Community[1]
			Environment and Ecology	Justice and Law	Housing	Other	Unspecified	
Chemicals	1.1	2.4	8.1	0.3	0.1	4.4	1.9	18.2
Electrical machinery and equipment	0.7	2.8	0.3	0.1	0.2	3.1	0.1	7.3
Food, beverage and tobacco	0.6	2.2	0.7	0.4	0.1	4.5	2.9	11.4
Machinery, nonelectrical	3.0	2.4	0.8	0.5	0.3	4.1	1.6	12.8
Paper and like products	0.4	1.9	23.3	0.1	0.4	8.9	—	34.9
Petroleum and gas[a]	2.0	6.0	1.4	0.6	1.0	5.1	2.9	19.0
Pharmaceuticals	1.1	2.4	0.4	0.4	0.2	2.0	1.5	7.9
Other manufacturing[b]	1.0	3.7	1.0	0.6	0.7	1.4	0.4	8.8
Printing and publishing	0.6	2.7	0.3	0.2	0.2	5.5	6.9	16.3
Textiles and apparel	0.8	2.9	0.4	0.4	—	2.7	4.3	11.5
Transportation equipment[c]	3.5	2.6	0.4	0.4	0.2	2.4	0.5	9.9
Total: Manufacturing	1.3	3.1	2.0	0.3	0.3	3.8	1.6	12.5
Banking	1.7	4.2	1.1	0.5	1.9	1.7	2.8	13.9
Business services[d]	2.2	4.8	0.1	0.1	0.1	9.4	—	16.7
Finance	9.6	1.7	0.4	0.2	0.6	6.6	8.3	27.3
Insurance	1.3	4.5	18.6	1.7	0.5	5.0	1.3	32.9
Retail and wholesale trade	0.4	4.4	0.1	0.3	0.5	4.3	10.1	20.1
Telecommunications	0.7	1.6	0.1	0.4	*	1.2	7.5	11.4
Transportation	—	0.1	*	0.1	1.0	7.6	0.4	9.2
Utilities	0.8	4.1	0.6	0.3	0.2	3.7	7.0	16.8
Total: Nonmanufacturing	1.5	3.5	4.4	0.6	0.6	3.4	5.2	19.2
Total: All Companies	1.3	3.2	2.7	0.4	0.4	3.7	2.5	14.2

[1]See footnotes on page 54.

Table 18: Beneficiaries of Company Support, 1987—Companies Grouped by Industry Class (with at least five cases in each) (continued)

Industrial Classification	Other Total Other[1]
Chemicals	6.5
Electrical machinery and equipment	29.3
Food, beverage and tobacco	6.8
Machinery, nonelectrical	3.4
Paper and like products	7.8
Petroleum and gas[a]	2.2
Pharmaceuticals	24.3
Other manufacturing[b]	2.8
Printing and publishing	3.7
Textiles and apparel	4.1
Transportation equipment[c]	2.8
Total: Manufacturing	13.6
Banking	7.8
Business services[d]	0.7
Finance	4.7
Insurance	3.2
Retail and wholesale trade	1.6
Telecommunications	1.7
Transportation	1.2
Utilities	5.2
Total: Nonmanufacturing	3.7
Total: All Companies	11.0

[1]See footnotes on page 54.

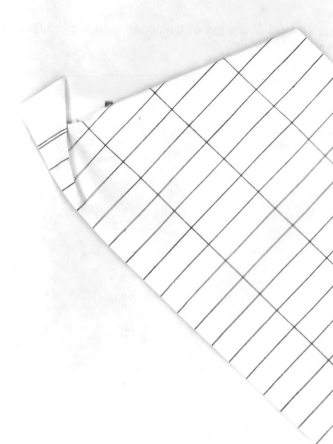